Sales Seduction

WHY DO YOU
SAY YES?

SALES
SEDUCTION

RHONDALYNN KOROLAK

Cover Design by Chameleon Print Design
Typeset by BookPOD
Printed and bound in Australia by BookPOD

This book is available for purchase from:-
www.imagineeringnow.com

A Cataloguing-in-Publication is available from the National Library of Australia

ISBN: 978-0-9805578-6-2   (pbk.)
eISBN: 978-0-9805578-7-9   (ebook)

Contents

PART ONE
7 Stimuli That Charm the Old Brain

CHAPTER 1

Why Is Everything All About YOU?...13

CHAPTER 2

Is Your Message Stimulating or Mind-Numbing? 19

CHAPTER 3

Are You Speaking Greek to the Reptilian Brain? 27

CHAPTER 4

Do You Make It Safe for Your Prospects to Buy From You?........35

CHAPTER 5

Is Your Message Complete or Half-Baked? 43

PART TWO
7 Steps That Help Your Prospects to Say "Yes"

PART THREE
7 Impact Boosters That Amplify Your Influence

CHAPTER 18

CHAPTER 19

CHAPTER 20

CHAPTER 21

Why Do You Say "Yes"?

Let me tell you a story about a friend of mine.

A few years ago, Molly worked in a small gourmet food store. One day a new customer walked into the store, made a quick purchase, then left. As he did so, Molly was so taken by this man that she found herself unable to move. It was only the laughter of her workmate Stella that jolted her back to reality.

I saw Molly that night and she was very excited—far more excited than you would expect over a man she had met once, over the counter, and whom she knew nothing about other than his preference for camembert. Anyway, Molly made it clear that she was going to pursue this guy. She was going to find out as much as she could about him, and slowly but surely get to know him. Eventually, she convinced herself, she would work up the courage to ask him out.

Molly's enthusiasm wasn't dampened at all when I pointed out that, at the very least, the man in question had to come back into her shop at least once. "Oh, that will happen," she said. "I just know it."

All of this was very unusual for Molly. Normally she waited shyly to be asked out rather than make the first move. She often regaled me with stories of Stella, who seemed like quite the opposite: bright red lipstick, figure hugging dresses which accentuated her hourglass figure, a flirtatious personality—and with a new man on her arm most weekends.

I suggested, only half joking, that Molly could get Stella to give her a few pointers, but she laughed this off. "I'd rather keep this man for more than a weekend," she said.

When I next saw Molly her eyes were shining and at first I thought she had succeeded in her goal. Not quite, at least not yet, but things were moving in the right direction. The man in question had returned to the store, more than once, and Molly had managed to strike up a bit of conversation with him. She knew more of his likes and dislikes and was now finding that he often asked her advice about a cheese selection or something else from the deli. Importantly, she had found that his good looks were matched by very pleasant behavior and manners—and she knew that he was single. She thought it was only a matter of time before she'd be brave enough to ask him out.

One evening I was passing Molly's store and dropped in to see her. We chatted for a few minutes and then suddenly Molly stared at the door and went quiet. I turned to see a smart looking man step inside—carrying a bunch of flowers. I thought for a moment that Molly was going to collapse in a fit of nerves. He smiled at Molly, and then proceeded to walk straight past us to the back of the store. There, he gave the bunch of flowers to Stella.

Have You Mastered the Art of Seduction?

Molly laughs when I tell this story now. But at the time, she wasn't laughing at all. She was crushed when the object of her affection had fallen so quickly and completely for the subtle feminine wiles of Stella. It didn't make sense to Molly's rational mind—she thought she had done all the right things to "woo" him. She had asked him lots of questions, spent time getting to know his likes and dislikes, and she had even become a trusted advisor, but none of it worked. None of it had the desired effect of getting him to notice her and ask her out.

It took a long time for her to understand that the art of seduction has little to do with conscious thought and rational processes. It has to do with primitive instincts and innate triggers that happen below the surface of your awareness. You become attracted to certain people (and messages) and you feel compelled to act, oftentimes long before you have the opportunity to think things through clearly. Fortunately or unfortunately, thinking takes place long after the decision has already been made.

Surprisingly, the dilemma you face in marketing and selling your products or services has a whole lot more in common with Molly and her story than you might think. You and I say "Yes" to things every single day without actually thinking about it. In fact, you may have even recently said "Yes" to something and wondered why you did so, hours or days later.

In this book you will discover exactly why you say "Yes" and what specifically compels you to decide and take action (as opposed to needing to "think about it"). And in the process you will also unlock the secret to transform your sales and marketing messages. You see, in reality, there is not much difference between seduction, in the traditional sense of boy-meets-girl, and Sales Seduction in your job or business. It doesn't matter what you are selling or whom you are selling it to. Every one of us is selling something—a product, an idea, a service, a lifestyle, or even (as Molly found out) yourself!

Why Does Your Brain Sometimes Struggle to Decide?

Thankfully, we know a lot more now than we did a few years ago about why it is that you say "Yes" to some messages and "No" or "I don't know" to others. In fact, until recently most of the research that was done in this area by marketing firms was highly subjective—it involved subjects being shown several messages and then being asked what they liked about each and whether or not they would consider taking up any of the offers. And as you might suspect, it is impossible to rely with any degree of accuracy on what someone says they might do.

Medical science and some high-tech equipment called fMRI (or functional magnetic resonance imaging) and EEG (electroencephalogram) have provided a more objective and deeper understanding of how your brain processes sensory input and makes decisions. We now have much greater insight into the three major sections of the brain and how each performs different functions as you think, feel, and act your way through each day. While each of these distinct parts of your brain is constantly communicating with and influencing each other, each piece performs a very specific role. And as you might suspect, only one of them is responsible for decision making.

Rather than just relying on the verbal responses of marketing survey subjects, neuroscientists have monitored and measured the area of the brain that lights up when decisions are made and correlated these findings back to the specific stimuli in the messages that triggered them. That is how we know that:

Your new brain (or neocortex) THINKS. This is where you process data.

Your middle (or mammalian) brain FEELS. This is where you perceive emotions.

Your old (or reptilian) brain DECIDES. This is where you act and react.

So when your customer says, "I need to think about it," the part of the brain that your message is triggering is the new brain (or neocortex). This part of the brain lights up when you are processing words, numbers, colors, making spatial comparisons, or looking for data. This is the one part of the brain that is unique to us as human beings and it is the last to form in the womb. In a nutshell, this part of your brain THINKS and when it does so, it uses up tons of energy—which prolongs the decision making process.

Now thinking may not seem like a big deal to you but it is for your brain. In fact, power conservation is a crucial driver. Your brain contains 1 million kilometers of interconnected fiber and over 100 *billion* neurons, and they all demand energy from your body. While your brain only weighs 6kg (which is small relative to your total body weight), it demands and consumes 25% of your body's total energy to fuel all this activity. Because of this extraordinary consumption, your brain is hardwired to conserve energy when and where it can. One of the ways it does this is to NOT rely on the thinking part of your brain to make decisions.

So if you want to drag out the process of getting your purchaser to decide, you definitely want to make sure that he uses his new brain and does a lot of thinking. Give your audience lots of words, numbers, graphs, lists of features and benefits, talk about your competition, and list all of your awards and accreditations—and your customer will NOT decide but he will do a whole lot of thinking and take up more of your valuable time in the process.

Many experts and business owners make the mistake of thinking that decisions take place in the middle or mammalian brain. This is the part of the brain that you and I share with every other warm blooded creature on the planet and it is where we process emotions and feel. But it is not where you decide. While emotions are important and have an influence on the ultimate decision, a decision will not take place quickly if only this part of the brain is engaged or triggered.

So where do you decide? At the top of your spinal cord, there is a collection of neurons—commonly referred to as the old (or reptilian) brain. All bodily functions that take place below the level of consciousness emanate from this part of your brain. You may like to think of it as your fight-or-flight brain—the part that is responsible for ensuring that you survive. It houses the amygdala—the chemical factory that regulates emotional reactions and your body's responses. And it is the part of the brain that lights up when you DECIDE. In fact, it lights up before you have conscious awareness (in your new brain) that you have even made a decision because it "sees" things as much as 500 milliseconds faster than the neocortex.

> **KEY POINT**
> **This part of your brain is automatic—the old brain**
> **does not think, it can only DECIDE and ACT.**

It is always at work scanning the environment for information of value to your survival. In order to help your prospects use the least amount of brain energy in processing your message and trigger a quick decision, you must stimulate and appeal to the old brain.

As it turns out, the old brain is very aptly named—seeing as how it can be traced back 450 million years. A significant amount of research exists to prove that the old brain dominates the decision making process. As explained by world renowned neuroscientists Robert Ornstein and Leslie Hart, the old brain is a primitive, survival-focused organ which processes sensory input much more quickly than the other parts of the brain, and as such, it determines which decisions will be accepted and acted upon.

It is indeed the oldest part of your brain—it was the first part to form and develop in the womb and it is also the same brain that we share with all other animals that have a spine and vertebrae (including, but not limited to, reptiles). As such, many people still refer to the fight-or-flight center of the brain as the reptilian brain. This part of your brain is concerned solely with your survival, and it has not evolved or adapted radically in millions of years. What this means is that survival-related functions dominate the decision making process because the amygdala exerts a domineering influence on the other parts of the brain.

From an evolutionary standpoint, only 6 million years separate human beings and the primate ancestor that we share with the apes. The word "only" is used deliberately here because 6 million years is a very short period of time when contrasted with the age of the old brain itself. What this means is that we as humans essentially share our genetic make-up and old brain with chimpanzees and monkeys—and that part of the brain is primarily driven by visual cues and primitive instincts. There simply has not yet been enough time (from an evolutionary point of view) for the old brain to adapt to communication, technology, and cognitive reasoning.

Only 40,000 years ago, humans were still communicating via groans and gestures. After the creation of words, it still took another 30,000 years before the written word was invented. The part of your brain that decides is 45,000 times older than language and writing. Neuroscience has proven that it struggles to process both.

Can You Speak the Language of Seduction?

So, you might be sitting there thinking, *"How is it even possible to influence and convince this primitive part of the brain to respond to my sales and marketing message?"* If the old brain cannot understand language, how are you going to help your customers to decide and say "Yes"?

If you merely go out and purchase one of the more than 14,000 sales and marketing books or programs that claim to have the best or most effective techniques, you will likely improve your results only marginally, here and there. Why is that?

It is too easy for you to get swept up and distracted by the "process" or the sales and marketing vehicle. You could get lost in complex models, caught up in channel management strategy, or place too much emphasis on closing techniques (or calls to action) that are designed to make your audience think they must decide now. While some of these techniques may work for some people, some of the time, they are not reliable or predictable because most of them are designed to trigger the wrong part (the thinking part) of your customer's brain. The more complicated the system, the more likely it is that you will put your purchaser to sleep, or worse, overwhelm the decision making part of his brain and cause him to have to "think about it".

In order to captivate the attention of and compel the old brain to react positively to your message, you must first learn to do one thing—**speak the language of the reptilian brain**.

All of the strategies and tactics contained in those other books and programs are of no use to you unless you first learn to speak the language of the true decision maker—the old brain. What I am about to share with you in this book has the power to transform your results exponentially—because it will simplify your message, reduce the amount of time it takes your audience to decide, and it will work no matter which medium or channel you choose to communicate it in.

The bad news is, of course, that the language of the old brain is primitive and restrictive. The good news is that it is incredibly simple, easy to remember, and when used correctly it will produce predictable and reliable results with your audience.

How Can You Help Your Prospects to Decide?

In this book, I am going to show you a simple way to do what Stella did naturally: appeal to the old brain in the only language it understands, and help your prospects to say "Yes" (more quickly) to your product or service.

If your marketing message is getting lost or falling on deaf ears, this information will help you grab attention and increase recall.

If your sales cycle is currently taking too long, this book will accelerate the process and save you time and money.

If your sales or marketing message is putting your prospects to sleep, this insight will help you get to the point.

If your would-be customers need to "think about" doing business with you, this knowledge will help you trigger a decision.

To do this I am going to take the key findings from neuroscience and the success stories of my clients and boil them down to a simple, step-by-step process that you can use to captivate attention, accelerate the sales process, close more business, and trigger decisions. Not only will I explain what works and what doesn't, but I will also help you apply it to your message, your product or service, and your customers. Specifically, I will cover the following:

- 7 Stimuli That Charm the Old Brain

- 7 Steps That Help Your Prospects to Say "Yes"

- 7 Impact Boosters That Amplify Your Influence

Once you see and understand the simple, automatic process that your brain follows whenever it makes a decision, it will be easier for you to speak to your customers in the language they need to hear. By mastering the 7 Stimuli, 7 Steps and 7 Impact Boosters, you will have everything you need to re-engineer your customer's decision making process. You will be able to go back to the beginning, and rework what you say and how you say it in order to influence a speedy decision in your favor.

And the best part about Sales Seduction is that you do not need to compromise your integrity or your ethics to improve your results. With Sales Seduction you will not fall into the trap of feeling that you need to hard sell your audience, make your message more elaborate, spend more money getting it out there, or use tactics that are designed to trick them into feeling that they need to "buy it now".

The 7 Step Sales Seduction Process has been put together for one simple reason—to make it easier for your customer to understand your core message. When you make it easy for him to see and grasp it with his old brain, he is much more likely to make a decision and he will on some level appreciate the fact that you have not wasted his time and energy with stuff that made him think way too hard.

And before we move on to explore the 7 Stimuli That Charm the Old Brain, I want to come back to the story that started this whole discussion. As you know, Molly and Stella had two very different ways of appealing to the mysterious male customer. Molly used the quite rational approach of getting to know the man, finding out what interested him, and working toward asking him out over a long period of time. Stella used another method entirely—something that got straight through and spoke clearly and effectively to the man's reptilian brain. In the end, Stella won. This book will help you unravel HOW she did it and help you to apply the insights to your message.

> **KEY POINT**
> In order to captivate the attention of your audience and compel them to say "Yes" to your message, you must learn to speak the language of the reptilian brain.

PART ONE

7 Stimuli That Charm the Old Brain

As you now know, the part of your brain that decides is an automatic mechanism, the sole purpose of which is to keep you safe and alive. It is a primitive organ with its own language, and as you are about to discover, the key to becoming highly skilled at speaking reptilian lies in mastering the 7 Stimuli that influence the reptilian brain. And remember, these 7 Stimuli are the only ones that hold the power to captivate the attention of the old brain and motivate it to decide.

CHAPTER 1

Why Is Everything All About YOU?

Old Brain Stimulus #1—Is Your Message Self-Centered?

It's always a bit surreal when someone you haven't seen for years suddenly appears in a newspaper. But there she was—Carol, an old client—with her smiling face staring at me from a fairly large advertisement in the local paper.

I looked at the ad for some time. It concerned me for a couple of reasons. First, when I had last seen Carol the last thing she would have been doing was paying for advertising. Her beauty salon was busy, with a growing list of regular clients; all the growth she needed was happening via word of mouth. Second, Carol had obviously invested a reasonable amount of money in this ad, yet it really wasn't doing a great job of promoting her business. In fact, it was fairly forgettable.

I remembered that Carol had always been pretty good at taking advice on board, so I thought I might drop in and see her.

The next day I walked into Carol's salon and was surprised to find that it had little of the buzz that I remembered. Carol and one other hair stylist were working with clients, but other than that the remaining eight chairs were empty. Nevertheless, Carol's eyes lit up and she greeted me with a warm hug.

"It's that new shopping center down the road," Carol told me after we retreated to her office a little later. "All my clients shop there, and while they're there they seem to be drawn in by the discounted haircuts offered by the two franchises in there. It's really frustrating, but I don't know what I can do to get them back. Running the ad was the only thing I could think of that would remind them that I am here—that's why I put my photo in it, even though I didn't really want to. But it hasn't really worked—it brought in maybe one or two new clients. And it doesn't seem to have brought back any of my previous regulars."

"I can see your logic," I said, "and I don't think there is anything wrong with using advertising, but I think there is a problem with your message."

I pulled out a copy of Carol's ad and held it up. Apart from the photo of Carol, which was quite nicely done, the advertisement contained a long list of her salon's services: hair styling, cuts, colors, waves, plus additional things like make-up and manicures. It was jam-packed full of features and benefits.

"The biggest problem with this ad," I went on, "is that it's all about *you*. It's not about your customers. The fact is that your customers—at least those former regulars whom you'd most like to get back—already know what you do. What they need is some reason to come back, something that goes beyond just reminding them of who you are and what you can do. Something that is attractive to them and will make them want to return."

"So ... should I be offering a discount? That would be about them, wouldn't it?"

"Possibly, but that would only reinforce the price war the franchised salons used to lure them away in the first place. What if you went a step beyond that? What could you offer that is even more valuable in your customers' eyes than a discount?"

As we chatted for a bit longer Carol started to remember what it was that she had always prided herself on: no client had ever left her salon in tears over a bad haircut or color. She offered a money back guarantee and, thankfully, no customer had ever needed to claim it. Carol and her team listened very carefully to the needs of each customer and had put systems in place to ensure that mistakes and oversights just didn't happen. If the client was unhappy for any reason, they took the time to make it right. They maintained careful notes on each client about their preferences and special requirements, which sped up their service but also made the customers feel important and valued. And they had extensive experience fixing the errors made by amateurish stylists at the other hair salons.

I asked Carol if the clients of the franchise salons were likely to get that sort of professional service.

"Not at all," she said. "At $39 a haircut, they're lucky if they are able to have the same hairdresser twice before another recent graduate is given the job. And those places are all about moving people through quickly, so there isn't even much time for a chat."

"I think perhaps it's time to remind your old clients about the downside of getting a cheap haircut or color treatment," I said. "How about we mock up another ad—one that's all about your customer."

KEY POINT
The most resonant word in the English language is 'you'.

People love to talk about themselves and they love to be shown how a product or service will take away their pain, keep them safe, or make their lives better. Like it or not, self-centeredness is one of the core stimuli that drive your decisions and behavior: it is a fundamental trait, hardwired into the reptilian—or "old"—part of your brain.

Self-centeredness is not all bad. It keeps you alive: when you encounter danger, your old brain kicks in—even before you are consciously aware of the danger—and has you moving out of harm's way. A milder version of the same thing happens when you are watching the news. When you see something bad on the news you can't help but think, somewhere in the back of your mind, *"I'm glad that wasn't me."* You will probably have plenty of sympathy for the victim, but no matter how much you feel for them, your hardwired survival instinct is pleased that you're okay.

It is because of this innate self-centeredness that you should always focus 100% of your sales and marketing messages on how your products and services will cure the pain of your customer or keep her safe. Your sales or marketing message should not focus on you or the features and benefits of your products and services (even if that's what everyone else is doing). Every time your prospect reads an ad or hears your message, they will be asking themselves, at least subconsciously, *"What's in it for me?"* It's your ad's job to answer that question in a way your potential customer can quickly grasp, and decide and act upon.

Take some time today to think about how you can apply this critical principle to your ads, your website, your business card, your next email, or even your packaging. Your customers are not thinking about you—they are thinking about their own survival and whether or not you can cure their pain or keep them safe. How can you reframe your message and let her know that you understand her greatest fears or challenges and that you can heal them? To the extent that you do this well up-front, she will listen to whatever it is you have to say.

If you remember, Carol's first newspaper advertisement was all about herself, her salon, and her features and benefits. And pretty much no one took any notice of it.

Her new ad was quite different. We used a simple headline and a small amount of text focused on the client, her pain, and her need for a solution:

Regret Your $39 Haircut?

Don't despair. Our expert stylists can fix it for you today. Even better ... save money and tears next time by coming to us first. We offer a 100% money back guarantee and, thankfully, none of our customers have ever had to use it.

And as a compelling image, we found a photo of a woman who was pulling at her hair in distress over the terrible cut and color she just received at a competitor's salon.

When I rang Carol a month later she was over the moon. The new ad generated a 26% increase in traffic and sales. A number of regulars had already returned and after a couple more weeks nearly half of her original customers had been back in for a cut or color treatment. They all, she told me, had tales of woe about what they had experienced at the salons in the shopping center. And they all thanked Carol for reminding them why it pays to get it done right the first time.

Over time Carol's client-focused ad actually helped her attract more new customers via word-of-mouth referrals as well. She found that her clients were telling others about the amazing results they were getting and many of them spoke about how much they related to the photo of the distressed woman in Carol's ad.

KEY POINT
Never waste your marketing money telling potential customers about *you*. 100% of your message should focus on your prospect or customer, and how your solution will cure her pain, keep her safe, or make her life better.

Is Your Message Stimulating or Mind-Numbing?

Old Brain Stimulus #2—Does Your Message Have Enough Contrast?

"I know it's what I want to do. I just don't know how to make it work!" Sam turned her attention to the ceiling and held it there for some time before looking back at me.

For six years now Sam had worked successfully as an owner-operator, mostly doing commercial photography for cookbook publishers and the like while also maintaining a clientele for studio portraits. "It"—the thing she now wanted to do—was a return to wedding photography. While she understood the pitfalls of dealing with emotionally tense clients, she missed the creative challenge of capturing private wedding moments on film.

The problem was that in the few years since she had last been involved in that part of her industry, the wedding photography scene had become a whole lot more competitive.

"When I look through all the fat, glossy wedding magazines, all the photography ads look the same. They all show off a couple of nice images taken in perfect light, and they all claim to be reliable and creative and ... blah, blah, blah. What are you smiling at?"

I couldn't help smiling simply because the more Sam described the sameness of the wedding photography advertisements she'd been looking at, the more her solution should have been obvious to her.

"So you want to stand out from the other photographers, not waste your money on an ad that looks just like all the others?" I asked.

"Exactly. But I still don't see why that is funny."

"It's not funny, but the solution will be fairly obvious once you recognize it. All you need to do is come up with a message that is markedly different— something which shouldn't be hard to do if they're all the same," I said.

I explained that Sam was exactly right in her determination to avoid doing "more of the same". The problem all these photographers had was that none of them stood out from the others—there was no *contrast*. There was nothing to grab a bride-to-be's attention as she flicked through a magazine's pages.

"Okay," she said. "That makes sense. Let's toy with the idea and see where we end up. Maybe an ad without any photography?"

"Perhaps, though pictures are incredibly powerful and persuasive with the part of your prospect's brain that decides," I said. "Let's step back a moment. What is an upcoming bride's greatest fear?"

"Probably the groom not turning up, though that doesn't happen very often ... and there wouldn't be much I could do about that anyway." Sam paused for a moment. "I think the biggest fear a bride would have on her wedding day is that the skies will be pouring down rain—that her hair and make-up will be ruined and they'll have to resort to pictures taken at the reception room, or worse, posed in a boring studio. In her mind, the worst scenario she could imagine is to end up with photos that she hates or ones that look like everyone else's."

This sounded promising. From what Sam had described, none of her competitors gave any indication that they would provide anything other than the standard, staged studio shots on a wet day.

"What if you were to use that angle? Could you offer a wet weather guarantee that you'll offer a reshoot on another day in the event of rain?" I asked.

Sam didn't think that would work—it would be too costly and in many cases logistically difficult. "Suit hire and everything that goes along with getting the bride ready again is just too much work for everyone," she said. "However ..." Sam got up and went over to a bookcase full of photo albums. She scanned the shelves for a moment before pulling down a very large volume. When she came back she set the book down on the table and turned over a few pages. "Yes, here it is."

What Sam showed me were some truly stunning and memorable wedding photos. They were beautifully crafted treasures and they were also different for one obvious reason: they had all been taken in pouring rain.

"This was probably the wettest wedding I ever had to shoot," she said. "It rained, heavily, for the whole day. But I was determined not to let the bride and groom down, so we got creative. Before the ceremony I went to a golfing shop and found two of the biggest, whitest umbrellas I could find, plus a couple of other props. We found some interesting locations on the golf course, and I got the couple to take the umbrellas and stand out in the middle of the rain. With my assistant's help, we were able to get these unique and captivating pictures. The couple, who met on that very golf course, were ecstatic when they saw we captured their special moments in time."

Sam didn't really need my help after she reached this point. It became quite clear to her that the way she could present herself differently was with a wet weather guarantee: not a guarantee to reshoot or retouch, but a guarantee to take unforgettable pictures no matter what the weather. With the help of a graphic designer she produced a split photo ad: on the left, a bridal party attempting unsuccessfully to outrun a terrible downpour on the way to the church, and on the right, her photo of the couple who celebrated their love and playfulness on the golf course in the rain. The text below the ad simply read:

> *If the weather is unforgettable for all the wrong*
> *reasons, we promise to make your photos and lifelong*
> *memories unforgettable for all the right reasons.*

When I last spoke to her, she said it was working a treat—especially in the traditionally "slow" wet period over winter.

What Sam had inadvertently discovered is the importance of another reptilian brain stimulus: contrast. Your old brain is constantly scanning the environment for contrast. It notices stark differences—big against small, hard against soft, dark against light, rough against smooth. It does this because identifying contrast quickly means it can detect threats, take action, and keep you alive.

KEY POINT
The old brain uses contrast to help it make
rapid decisions and keep you alive.

Take the example of a frog—if you drop a frog into a pot of boiling water on the stove, it will immediately jump out to save itself. That's the usefulness of the old brain in action. But if you put that same frog into a pot of water at room temperature, it will stay put—even if that water is slowly brought up to the boiling point. It's a perfect example of how important contrast is to the part of your brain that decides.

If there is significant contrast, your old brain is motivated and you will feel compelled to take action now. You won't feel the need to make a list, evaluate the pros and cons, and worry where you will find the money. The old brain will make a decision now and the rest of your brain may ask questions later.

However, if you don't see enough contrast, even though the threat is real and imminent, you will not sense any urgency to make a decision and jump before it is too late. Instead, you will kick up the information to the thinking part of your brain where you will source and evaluate data, create a spreadsheet, research the competition online, or create objections. Meanwhile, you could very well be losing money, losing sleep, losing competitive advantage, or worse (like our frog in the example above) boiling to death!

In this same way your customer needs to feel the difference between your solution, your competitor's solution, doing it themselves, or doing nothing.

Have you ever stopped to ask yourself whether your current message makes it clear to your audience what will happen if they don't choose your solution? Isn't this more powerful than just trying to convince them why they should pick you? Could just this one simple shift in your approach light a fire under their butts and motivate them to decide?

At the end of the day, if you want to sell a bucket of water, a smoke alarm, or a fire extinguisher, should you spend 80% of your time talking about features and benefits or should you just light a fire? Which approach do you think is more effective at curing indecision?

If your prospects can't see the difference on your brochure, your website, your email, or your sales pitch, they don't have to decide. It's as simple as that.

Now rest assured, they will continue to be in pain when they don't decide and you are actually doing them a great disservice by allowing their pain to drag on and on. In contrast, when you show them something they need that stands out—i.e. there is a significant gap between where they are and where they want to be—they feel compelled to act to remove their pain now. The more contrast you present, the easier you make it for your customer's old brain to decide.

> **KEY POINT**
> **In order to create contrast and trigger a fast decision, you must stand out. Your customer needs to feel the difference between your solution, your competitor's solution, doing it themselves, or doing nothing.**

From a marketing or sales perspective, contrast is vital because it triggers a decision by the old brain. Where there is no contrast between two competing suppliers, the old brain can't make a decision—just like the frog—and the information is passed up to the new brain for evaluation. When your customer tells you that he needs to think about it, what he is really saying is that you haven't provided enough contrast for him to make a decision now. Once he begins to apply rational thought to the process, you can bet that he will create a spreadsheet, create objections, research your competitors on the internet, and start to question your price.

If your prospects cannot clearly see the difference in the solution you are offering, they don't have to decide. When you show them something that they desperately need and your solution stands out, the old brain will kick in automatically to compel them to act to remove their pain. The more contrast you demonstrate in your solution, the easier you make it for your prospects to decide now.

Sam was able to stand out and differentiate her services by positioning herself as the wet weather wedding photographer. The contrast in her message, and the guarantee, not only made her easy to spot, but also addressed her clients' greatest fear—a wedding day ruined by rain. It was more than enough to get her phone ringing off the hook and most of her leads were already well on the way to being convinced she was the only choice for them.

It is also worth noting that Sam didn't call herself "one of the best wet weather photographers" but rather "*the* wet weather photographer". In order to stand out and provide sharp contrast you need to be the best at what you do. There is no point claiming to be "one of the few companies that does X" or "one of the top five companies that does Y". In doing so, you are essentially instructing your potential customers to go out and investigate how you rank against your competitors. This is why it is so critical to find an area where your customers are in pain and identify a solution that you can provide better than anyone else, one that is clearly different and valuable.

KEY POINT

No contrast = no decision. If there is no clear difference between you and your competitors in an area where your prospects have pain, you are inviting them to keep researching alternatives, thinking about it, and worrying about the price. Find a distinct point of difference that cures your customers' pain and then own that space in your market.

Are You Speaking Greek to the Reptilian Brain?

Old Brain Stimulus #3—Is Your Message Concrete or Tangible Enough for a 6-Year-Old?

I always get a lot of satisfaction out of talking to long-term clients, especially people like Jason, whom I've known since he first went into business on his own. Jason is a domestic electrician. His wife works part-time on some of the administration and he has the occasional apprentice sidekick, but other than that, he is the business. And that's just the way he likes it, which probably explains the smile on his face every time I see him.

Jason and I still catch up at least twice a year, sometimes a bit more often when he's trying to make a change to some aspect of his business. Like recently, when he called me to say he wanted some help with attracting "a better type of client". His Yellow Pages ad was coming due and he wanted to tweak it to incorporate some more information and some of his recent qualifications. This, he thought, would raise his profile a bit and get him larger, higher paying jobs and less tiny jobs like changing a light bulb or power point.

When I pulled up outside Jason's home, the first thing I noticed was the outside of his van was getting quite crowded with logos of various suppliers he used and accreditations he had gained. There were memberships with this and that organization, and approval from various professional bodies that probably meant nothing to a layperson; it looked as though Jason must have applied for just about every certification on offer.

When I mentioned this to him, he didn't look as proud of himself as I expected. "I've worked really hard to get all those badges," he said, "mostly because I thought it would help me in my effort to attract more lucrative work. But they're not really working. I think people aren't noticing them on the van because they are too small, which is why I want to add them to my Yellow Pages ad as well."

Unfortunately, it was time to burst Jason's bubble. On his van, Jason had committed a very common mistake that many of you may find you have also made in the past. If he now went ahead with his plan of updating his Yellow Pages ad, he would be repeating that same blunder again. And it would be a costly one.

Contrary to what you might think, the mistake wasn't his choice to invest in a Yellow Pages ad. Jason had been keeping track for well over 14 months and had determined that almost 38% of his business came directly from his ad. In fact, his mistake was a bit harder to spot—in his efforts to build up his credibility and perceived expertise, Jason had confused his customers instead of making it easier for them to say "Yes". *More* information is not always better than *less*. Rather than telling potential customers what they needed to hear to make a decision, he had begun sharing a whole lot of stuff that didn't mean anything to them and wasn't relevant to what they needed.

I tried to break all this to Jason gently.

"Jason, what is it that your best customers like most about the work you do for them? And by best customers I mean those most like the ones you want to attract more of with your ads and signage."

"Well, a few things, I guess. They often comment on my reliability—I always turn up on time or I call to update them if I'm running late. That is rare in our industry, apparently. And my helpful advice would be the other main factor. Residential electrical issues have become more and more complicated—with people wanting home theatre systems, wireless computer networks, home automation, and solar panels. My clients find it all pretty confusing and they look to me for clear-cut advice. So I make a point of explaining things simply and clearly, in a way that they can understand. I also help them make the right choices about technology."

Here was my chance. "That's fantastic, Jason. So it shouldn't come as too much of a shock if I tell you that I don't think your van, or this new ad, communicate your solution to your potential customers as clearly as you convey it to your existing ones."

Jason looked a bit bewildered at this so I pressed on. "What you're doing with your customers is taking something that is complicated and making it simple. You're taking wires, switches and controls, and all that other stuff which the average person finds impossible to get a handle on, and you're making it clear and accessible—so much so that they feel they can see it, grasp it, and make sense of it. You're making it very tangible.

"But your advertising has the opposite effect. You are spending too much time and real estate on logos, awards, and accreditations that your prospects do not understand the significance of. At the same time, your important claims about things that you do better than anyone else—your reliability and expertise—are being lost. The only people who know about those are your existing customers who have already experienced them firsthand."

Jason's face lit up like a light bulb; I could tell that he was starting to get the message. "So all this effort to prove myself with credentials, supplier logos, features, and benefits has been a waste of time? Boy, have I missed the blinding obvious—the simple answer was right in front of me all along!"

Oftentimes the "obvious" in business is rarely obvious until it is pointed out to you. I went on to explain that neuroscience has shown that accreditations and awards alone have minimal persuasive effect on the old brain. To the part of your brain that decides, all proof is not created equal. In fact, logos and credentials are much less persuasive than virtually every other sort of "proof" you can offer—including customer stories (which are the most influential), demonstrations, data, and a clearly stated vision. Proof becomes even more important in Chapter 12 when we discuss the various ways that you can prove to your target audience that you can deliver on your claims.

As I've explained, your old brain doesn't like having to do a lot of work to decipher and understand the thousands of messages you are bombarded with throughout your day. In order to react quickly and keep you safe it must rely on instinct and automatic responses to all incoming signals. From a historical perspective, this is what kept our ancestors alive.

When applied to a modern day marketing context, this means that your old brain is much more likely to absorb and react to a message or signal that is easily understood—one that, say, a 6-year-old could understand. A more complicated message involving numbers, big words, unfamiliar concepts, jargon, graphs, and clutter will cause your prospect's old brain to switch off and kick the information up to the neocortex for thought, evaluation, and lots of processing.

> **KEY POINT**
> **In order to be effective and to be understood by the old brain, your message must be simple enough for a 6-year-old to comprehend.**

If you had to share your latest ad, brochure, or website with a 6-year-old right now, would she get it? Could you close the sale? Does your prospect have to do a whole lot of new brain thinking to "get it"?

If you've been making this classic mistake, what do you need to do to boil it down, right now, to something that a child could grasp and act upon? Where you can, eliminate fluff, big words, and jargon that doesn't mean anything to the old brain. When you make it easy for your prospects to "get it", you allow more time and opportunity for them to ask you *how* you do it.

You will definitely know when you have got your message wrong because your potential customers will simply turn off their decision making brains like switching off the lights in a room. Get your message right—simple and concrete—and they won't be asking whether or not they need your product or service, they'll be asking how and when they can get it.

From an old brain perspective, if your message is easy enough for a 6-year-old to see and grasp, you will close much more business because your customers will "get it" immediately and take action more often.

Now, this is not necessarily an easy task. Making your message simple and tangible takes time and effort. Most companies take the easy way out and err on the side of including anything and everything, hoping that something will work. Open a copy of the Yellow Pages and see for yourself—almost every tradesman in the book has provided a long list of awards, services, accreditations, and other "about us" material, rather than focusing on making their product or service tangible and easy to understand.

Look at it this way: if you don't invest your own time and effort up-front to make your message tangible and concrete, you are effectively asking your potential customers to do the hard work for you—to waste valuable brain power and effort to figure out why they should buy from you. In the end someone has to do the hard work—either you do it, or they will. Of course, asking them to do this hard work means that you risk losing them or extending the sales cycle because they can't make sense of your sales or marketing message. Does this sound like good use of your customers' valuable time and energy?

> **KEY POINT**
> Someone has to do the hard work. If you don't do it up-front, it means your customer has to do it in order to decide whether or not they should buy from you.

For Jason, this meant a significant rethink in terms of the way he communicated to customers and potential clients via print advertising and van signage. His main message was reduced to one that even a layperson could understand:

In the Dark?

We keep your lights on and help you make the right choice about all your electrical needs.

Once the Yellow Pages copy had been dealt with, he was up and running, translating the same message to his truck, his business cards, his quotation book, and his website. When we last spoke, Jason was surprised to report that a whopping 23% of his business was now coming from referrals and his website. Perhaps more interestingly, while others were abandoning the Yellow Pages, he was still getting 38–40% of his sales from his new and improved advertisement.

He didn't throw away his supplier logos, accreditations, and awards either—they still had value in their rightful place on page 5 of his website and the back door of his van—but he no longer saw them as the core reason why his customers chose him instead of his competitors.

> **KEY POINT**
> Don't take the easy way out. You should work harder up-front to craft your message than your prospect has to work in order to decipher it.

CHAPTER 4

Do You Make It Safe for Your Prospects to Buy From You?

Old Brain Stimulus #4—Does Your Message Sound Familiar?

Walking up the path toward what looked like a converted Victorian terrace house, I could smell Jeanette's practice well before I made my way inside. I'm not sure exactly what it was but it was that distinctive herbal aroma you tend to associate with health food stores and naturopathic clinics. It wasn't at all offensive, but it was distinctive. I entered the waiting room to discover everything pretty much as I expected: a safe pale blue color scheme, "spiritual" music playing quietly in the background, and an all-round feeling of wellness.

At the back of the long, narrow building was a small courtyard, which on this day was glowing in full late-afternoon sun. It was a wonderful spot for a meeting—a far cry from the sterile corporate boardroom I had just come from.

On the recommendation of a friend, Jeanette had contacted me for the usual reason—she wanted some help finding more clients, but Jeanette had a particular type of client in mind and an important reason for wanting to help them. It was quite clear after only a couple of minutes that this lady had substantial goals and a compelling vision. While on first impressions she was a calm, steady-as-she-goes type of woman, in line with her chosen profession, just below the surface was an entrepreneur on a mission.

It turned out that Jeanette had first come to naturopathy as a patient—a patient struggling with fertility issues. Years of traditional medicine had failed to yield any results for Jeanette and her partner, Adam. Wanting to avoid IVF if she could, Jeanette had approached a naturopath who specialized in fertility. A few months after she started the naturopathic regime, Jeanette discovered, at the age of 43, that she was pregnant—the natural approach worked a miracle. After she was blessed with a second child, Jeanette was convinced—so convinced, indeed, that she "bought the company", as the saying goes. She completed a Health Science degree majoring in natural medicine. After that she did advanced studies in naturopathy to treat fertility issues.

That was all over a decade ago and now, with both her children at school and a little more time available, Jeanette was determined to spread the message and cure for infertility as far and wide as she could. That meant, over time, having a bigger practice, or preferably a number of practices.

"The trouble with naturopathy," Jeanette told me, "is that we spend a lot of time preaching to the converted. Those who are already using natural medicines will come and see me without a second thought when they have trouble getting pregnant. But there is another whole group of people out there—both women and men—who won't come near an alternative clinic. They see natural medicine as quackery, don't trust it, and won't even give it a try.

"There are women out there suffering, many who could be helped by what I can do, but who are missing out on children altogether or going through the cost and pain of IVF unnecessarily. It frustrates the heck out of me that I can't convince them to at least come and see me once."

I gave Jeanette a minute to let her passion wind down before asking a few questions. "We're talking largely about couples here, I suspect?" I asked. "The decision to seek 'alternative' advice about fertility would usually be a joint one, wouldn't it?"

"Yes ... well it's certainly better when that is the case. Fertility 'constraints', for want of a better word, can lie with either the man or the woman. And I see where you're going—quite often we can have an existing patient who is keen to seek advice about fertility issues, but who cannot convince the partner to come in. But of course there are many couples where both are unwilling to try alternative medicine."

"And what do you think is the source of the resistance? Is it just one thing?" I asked.

Jeanette thought about this question for a moment. "I think there are probably many things, but the underlying problem most likely is fear of the unknown. Many are simply not comfortable with what they don't know. New clients and prospects often tell me that their resistance is due to fear and uncertainty—that if they understood naturopathy better, they would have been more likely to come in sooner. But I'm not entirely convinced— most people have little understanding of what their physician does, yet they're happy to go along with the doctor's advice and recommended treatment. The difference isn't fear or understanding—I think it comes down to familiarity."

Inadvertently, Jeanette had touched on a powerful stimulus that drives the decision making part of your brain: familiarity.

Your reptilian brain likes things it knows well or is familiar with because they feel safe. Remember, this part of your brain wants to keep you alive. By contrast, unfamiliar things represent a potential threat, so your old brain reacts swiftly to steer you away from them.

> **KEY POINT**
> A familiar person or message is a safe bet for the old
> brain. Remember, your old brain is constantly scanning the
> environment looking for things that might kill you.

Recognizing this trigger has provided the foundation for many sales and marketing techniques to build rapport—most notably the neuro-linguistic (NLP) practice of "matching and mirroring" in which the salesperson actively copies the body language of his prospect in order to get "in sync" with them on a deeply subconscious level. In a nutshell, we like to do business with people we like, and who are like us.

However, neuroscience supports the idea that we need to take this one step further. At its core what we are really talking about here is risk aversion. Psychologist Daniel Kahneman won a Nobel Prize for economics in 2002 for work he and colleagues did which demonstrated that people don't always make the rational buying decisions economists and businesses would like to believe. Rather, people give different weight to risks and gains. Put simply, people give more weight to potential losses—including loss of the familiar—than to potential gains. The psychology at play here has been used masterfully in quit smoking ads by The American Cancer Society, drink driving campaigns by the TAC (in Australia), and the "this is your brain on drugs" campaign by the US Food and Drug Commission.

> **KEY POINT**
> Your customers don't care what you have to give them, they care what they are losing because they don't yet have THE solution for their pain.

What this meant for Jeanette was that her message, which emphasized a very high potential gain (getting pregnant), was not enough to overcome the old brain of her potential clients who did not trust or understand her approach. She had not done enough to overcome the perceived risk of losing the familiar (i.e. of entering unfamiliar, unsafe territory).

One way of using the stimulus of familiarity to your advantage in your marketing message is to heighten the potential loss by pointing it out. This can work effectively with many different types of products and services. Jeanette could easily have done this by emphasizing the consequences of missing out on having children—by making the loss of not having children appear much greater than the risk of trying naturopathy. However, this approach would have had to be managed carefully in the context of Jeanette's business, to avoid scaring or alienating her potential patients. Another approach could have been to remove the danger of losing the familiar by finding a risk free way to prove that natural therapy was complementary to and endorsed by traditional medicine. She could easily have done this by offering a risk free assessment and aligning herself with sympathetic physicians.

But there was another option which had far more potential to draw customers to her practice and create a sense of safety and familiarity. By sharing her own personal, compelling story of fertility success, Jeanette could connect with new leads on common ground—she understood their struggle and had walked a mile in their shoes. She could also draw attention to the number of real customers, with similar fertility challenges, whose lives had forever been touched and enriched by the solution they received at her clinic.

Eventually Jeanette and I developed a marketing strategy that would help her achieve this. Jeanette found it a bit challenging at first because it was quite different from the norm in her industry. Even she was surprised at her level of fear around trying something new and different, but she could see the logic in persisting and pushing through it.

The strategy involved three things, all aimed at making her message and solution feel more familiar to potential clients who had no previous experience with alternative medicine.

First, she willingly shared her own story of facing and beating the fertility odds at age 43 and 45. Jeanette was quite candid on her website and in her marketing materials about the heartbreaking journey she and Adam faced when their medical doctor explained that it would be almost impossible for them to conceive. She also explained how she came to discover naturopathy and how her own experience differed quite dramatically from that of her friends who had persisted with IVF and been unsuccessful.

The second thing Jeanette did was completely overhaul her website. Instead of providing pages and pages of medical statistics and information designed to educate readers on the science of natural medicine, she made the entire web experience more personal and intimate. In addition to her own story, Jeanette added the photos, real names, and contact details of some of her clients. She let their stories of hope and success do the talking for her—she met her prospects where they were at and let them know that she understood their pain and had successfully worked with over 487 couples to create life.

Finally, and perhaps most interestingly, Jeanette visited a number of the local GPs in her area to discuss potential partnerships and referrals. Some were closed to the idea, but she found a number of the younger female doctors were open-minded and willing to refer patients Jeanette's way.

It's early days yet, but Jeanette tells me that she has seen a 12% increase in new clients and a 14% increase in referrals from existing, satisfied patients. By making her brand, her message, and her service more familiar to couples who were unsure about naturopathy, she effectively reduced the perceived risk of trying her solution and she is well on her way to her vision of opening up four more clinics in major cities.

It is worth noting that this important trigger for the old brain applies no matter what medium you use to communicate your sales or marketing message. If and when you meet your prospects face-to-face, what do you do in the first 60 seconds to let them know that they are in good hands and that it is safe to be with you? Your ability to put their old brain at ease quickly will exponentially increase your ability to influence them with your message.

This is also true for your website, brochures, emails, sales presentations, packaging, and social media interactions. Just because you are not speaking to them in the flesh, does not mean that you are off the hook. You must still find a concrete way to convey that you understand your prospects' pain and have experience helping clients exactly like them.

Do your existing materials make your leads feel safe or do they really give the distinct impression that you only care about your history, your product or service, and making the sale? Remember, once your prospect feels safe, he will let his guard down and be much more receptive to hearing about your solution.

KEY POINT
Unless your message is safe and familiar, your prospect won't let his guard down long enough to hear what you have to say.

Is Your Message Complete or Half-Baked?

Old Brain Stimulus #5—What Do You Need to Do to Get Closure?

I still have vivid memories of my first visit to Charlie's Hobby Shop—I remember how hard it was to find the sales counter among the stacks of boxes reaching all the way to the ceiling. There was so much dust and clutter that I felt overwhelmed by it all. Collecting had been Charlie's passion and probably the biggest reason he bought into his business. He had a passion for holding multiple copies of everything—"just in case"—and for always buying plenty of stock whenever the wholesaler had a special on offer. It was a passion that had nearly brought him undone until he figured out, with a bit of help from *Financial Foreplay*, how to free up some cash flow by finding a few practical ways to reduce his inventory.

Now Charlie was facing a new challenge. As he put it to me, "The youngsters aren't interested in things you have to do with your hands unless it involves video games or YouTube." More and more, his customers were getting older and they weren't being replaced by young blood.

Charlie was, admittedly, fairly "old school". He refused to stock computer games of any sort; train control boxes were about the only electronics he allowed on his shelves. But in other ways he had managed to bring himself into the twenty-first century. He used the internet a lot to both buy and sell stock. He also used it to stay in touch with enthusiastic hobbyists and other hobby store owners. And of late he'd even started using the internet to try and reach out to that elusive "younger" crowd.

He hired Lachlan, his smart young nephew, to help him set up an account on Facebook and add a "Fan" page for his business. He'd put a few specials up on that page but was starting to realize that just being on Facebook wasn't going to be enough. Now he had to get people to find his page and visit it regularly, and from there he had to get his page to encourage more people into his physical store.

"Lachlan says I should run some ads on Facebook to get more followers and he's happy to help me do that, but I think I need some advice as to what to put in those ads. I was going to advertise some regular specials, but I know it won't be of any use if my Facebook fans aren't interested in the products I feature." At this I noticed Charlie's shoulders sag a little, as if he couldn't understand how others would not share his passion. "And I'm basically at a loss to know what I can say that will get anything across to those young'uns."

His basic logic sounded pretty right, I told him. There wouldn't be much point investing in advertising, no matter how cheap, if the products weren't relevant or attractive. But I thought there might be another way of attacking Charlie's problem.

"Charlie, who are your best customers?"

Not one to be overly analytical, Charlie wasn't able to give me a very clear answer to this. But as we chatted about his typical customers it became clear that there were two main groups. One group was made up of people, mostly male, in their 40s or more, who weren't that different from Charlie—lifetime hobbyists who weren't going to let age and technology get in the way of their passion to build things with their hands. The other group were younger kids, mainly boys, probably no older than ten, who hadn't yet been completely devoured by the "online" or "screen culture". This group in particular seemed to be slowly disappearing.

"Presumably these young kids aren't spending their own money?" I asked.

"No, that's true. Some spend hard-earned pocket money but most of the time it's their fathers who do the buying. Often it's for birthdays or Christmas."

I asked Charlie if he'd ever chatted to the "lifetimers" or the dads about his predicament.

"Not a lot," he answered. "The hobbyist type isn't one to open up about personal stuff. There are a handful who hang around for a chat from time to time. Mostly they bemoan the 'screen culture' and fear that they are losing touch with their children. Some of them, especially the single dads, are really sad that they don't get much quality time with their sons and don't have many interests in common. Times have changed and it's not like it was when they were growing up and they visited the hobby shop with their own fathers on the weekends."

At this my ears pricked up. We talked a little more and it became apparent that we had isolated an important insight about Charlie's potential market—the lifetime enthusiasts were looking for a way to recreate the connection and closeness that they had had with their own fathers. If we could find a way to incorporate this into a Facebook ad and business page, we could ignite a revival of "father and son time" and sales. After a bit of work we came up with a strategy that would draw more dads into Charlie's store, with their sons in tow.

The good thing about Facebook ads is that, by limiting your offer to 135 characters and a small photo, they force you to focus on one simple message. Coincidentally, neuroscience has proven that your customer is more likely to remember and act upon your message if you present only one or two claims. Your customer's brain does not have the capacity to absorb a laundry list of factors and requests; it is far better to invest your time getting one clear point across than coming up with, say, half a dozen different benefits (or calls to action) and expecting your prospects to absorb them all.

> ### KEY POINT
> Less is more. To increase retention and action, pare down each marketing message or sales interaction to one or two key claims that are important to your customer.

As I've already explained, your brain is energy hungry. It is looking for any opportunity to conserve and rest—when it can, it powers itself down in the same way your computer does when switching to screensaver mode.

Michael Blanchette was so interested in this phenomenon that he undertook to measure the attention and retention capacity of the human mind. His research proved that your brain is actually very selective when it comes to retaining and recalling what it has heard. Since the old brain is primarily concerned with your physical survival, it will operate at near maximum alertness at the beginning and end of the tasks and interactions throughout your day. However, your level of attentiveness drops down to as low as 20% in the middle of each of those tasks and interactions. Essentially, once your old brain has scanned the environment and determined that it is safe for you to be where you are, it shuts down and takes a break.

Because of this energy consciousness, you'll find that you tend to remember the first and last of most things, putting out of your mind nearly everything else in between. It explains why you remember more clearly the start and end of a road trip while the middle part of the journey fades quickly from your mind. You likely recall your first home much more vividly than your third. And you definitely remember your first or last kiss better than your 112th!

The implications of this for your marketing and sales materials are significant. First and foremost, you need to put all your energy and emphasis on the first and last things that your potential customers will see or read. You need to capture attention and deliver your most powerful points up-front when your audience is most alert and receptive. Never start your marketing message or your presentation by introducing your brand, building your credibility, talking about your competitors, or providing a background summary. This strategy will put your customers to sleep and you risk having to deliver your most important claims and proof when customers are least likely to remember them.

If you have a strong opening message or claim, one that attracts and holds the attention of the old brain, it is better to repeat it again—further embedding it in your prospect's memory—than to introduce a completely new message or claim midway through your materials or meeting.

Finally, messages that paint a clear "before and after" picture in your prospect's mind are exponentially more effective than ones that do not. Remember, the old brain is hardwired to fire up and pay attention to the beginning and the end of everything. A clear "before and after" snapshot makes it easier for a potential customer to say "Yes" to your message because she can see the difference and imagine how it could change her life.

In the absence of closure (i.e. a clear "before and after"), your customer will be forced to send your data and information up to her new brain for processing, where she will take much more time "to think about it".

> **KEY POINT**
> The two most important parts of your presentation or marketing message are the beginning and the end. At the beginning, your sole purpose is to grab the attention of your audience and establish it is safe for them to be with you.

When Charlie and I did some work on his Facebook message, we concentrated on combining this concept of closure for the reptilian brain with the sense of nostalgia and connection his lifetimers had about the time they spent working on models and crafts with their own fathers.

For the Facebook ad, we used an image of a young boy seated at a wooden dining table putting together a model rocket with his adoring father. The text on the ad simply read:

When was the last time you did something together?

Using the Facebook ad demographic tools, Charlie was able to target this campaign specifically at men in their late 30s and early 40s—those most likely to have a young son and, therefore, most likely to connect with this message.

On Charlie's Facebook business page, this strong visual tale was repeated and reinforced with a split image: the first half being the original image, and the second half a more modern version of the photo, with the anecdote and call to action:

In the good old days, you called them rockets.
Today he calls them Transformers.

Isn't it time you reconnected with your son?

That was it—one message, simply illustrated and aimed directly at the hearts of the enthusiasts that Charlie most wanted to attract. He tripled his followers/leads in less than 45 days and increased sales by 18%.

Charlie's campaign successfully demonstrated how powerful the stimulus of closure is for the decision making part of the brain. He presented a very clear picture of his customer's life before and after his product and he was able to help his customer recreate the connection and closeness they had with their own fathers. Charlie applied this concept brilliantly with online advertising but it can easily be adapted and implemented by you in many other ways: to any other form of advertising, your next email campaign, a sales presentation, and even to important conversations with your team, suppliers, or family members.

When in doubt, tell your prospects a story.

All great salespeople, teachers, speakers, and marketers are good storytellers. What are the stories that you can retrieve or create which will give your audience a clear picture of how their life or business will be before and after your solution? What imagery and tales can you use to captivate the attention and interest of your prospects so that you maximize the time you have with them to deliver your solution?

Take a few moments now to review one of your recent communications. How many points did you bombard your prospect with and ask them to remember? Was that strategy effective, or is it possible that you could have accomplished more by saying less? Did you get to your most important claim in the first sentence or did you accidentally bury it like a hidden treasure somewhere in the middle?

Remember, it is impossible to keep your audience at 100% attention throughout. If you have a presentation or longer marketing message to deliver, you must build artificial beginnings and endings into your message in order to restart the brain and maximize the retention of important points. Consider using a photo or video to break up text, laying out material in separate boxes or pages to create the illusion of closure, or asking participants to stop periodically and write down the points they want to follow up.

KEY POINT
If it's not said at the beginning or the end, it
won't be recalled or acted upon.

Do Your Visuals Serve a Purpose or Do They Just Fill Space?

Old Brain Stimulus #6—Do Your Visuals Paint a Compelling Picture?

"It's just impossible to compete against these people. I can't live on $10 an hour!"

This was Tracy, a graphic designer, with a complaint I hear quite often from people like her—self-employed "creatives". The universal reach of the internet has made selling creative services a global proposition. A number of "auction" and freelance websites have appeared which make it easy for educated people in India, Bangladesh, and a host of other countries to bid for work against local designers like Tracy. And they bid low, sometimes very low, simply because, with very different lifestyles and standards of living, they can afford to.

The first question I ask clients like Tracy is simple—"Why are you trying to compete in this market?" The online sale of creative services is all about price, with quality and innovation a distant second and third. All the benefits of your skills, insight, and track record count for very little in this game.

It turned out that the real problem was that Tracy found she was no longer getting through to the type of clients she used to attract.

"They just don't get me," were her words. "When my work started to drop off a few months ago I decided to increase my marketing effort. I redid my website and since then I've tried all sorts of things. I've changed the wording on my website and brochures over and over again, but nothing ever seems to make any difference. The calls just aren't coming in. Then I discovered these overseas "auction" and freelance sites, and could only conclude that all the work is drifting overseas because it is so cheap. I can't survive and put food on the table at home for these rates, so I really don't know what to do."

I asked Tracy if we could have a look at her website together. I knew from my work with other creative design and web development businesses that there was, in fact, plenty of well-paying work out there—plenty of companies that valued local expertise and originality. Tracy's problem wasn't price, nor was it skills or ability. It had to be something else.

That something else became immediately apparent as soon as she opened her new website for me.

"Tracy, you're a graphic designer ... yes?"

She nodded, looking at me as if I was stupid.

"But your website's homepage is full of words. There is hardly an image on here, apart from that faint one in the background. It looks to me like you're working very hard to explain yourself in words when your most valuable asset is your ability to help others paint a compelling picture that draws customers to them."

We clicked through a few other pages and it was more of the same—lots of words and sales jargon with only a few small images here and there.

"I think," I went on, "you may have lost sight of the power of your artistic solution."

Neuroscience has proven that your brain is a visual beast. Somewhere between 80% and 90% of brain activity is associated with making sense of visual stimuli, and the brain processes these visual stimuli much more quickly—about 40 times more quickly—than it does auditory stimuli.

This makes perfect sense when you think about the role that visual cues played in the survival of our ancient ancestors—particularly the way in which the old brain reacted quickly to keep the cavemen out of the jaws of tigers and mammoths. The old brain is extraordinarily fast at processing these visual cues, "seeing" them in only 2–3 milliseconds and reacting to them almost instantaneously.

> **KEY POINT**
> **Your brain is hardwired to process visual cues and act**
> **before you have time to think things through carefully.**

In sharp contrast, it takes your new brain (or neocortex) a relatively snail-paced 500 milliseconds to process the exact same visual data. In many cases, your old brain and body have already made decisions and taken action based on what they have seen, long before you are consciously aware that you have seen anything at all! Since humans cannot rely on the slow processing speed of the new brain, you are hardwired to make decisions at the old brain level that are mostly based on visual input and instinctual responses. Your neocortex kicks in much later in the process to help you find data, proof, and justification for the gut decision you have already made.

This of course makes visual imagery one of the most powerful triggers you can harness and use to your marketing advantage. As they say, **a picture really is worth a thousand words.**

Of course, not all pictures are created equal. The visuals you use in your sales and marketing materials must mean something to the old brain of your prospect—they must have a "what's in it for me" (WIIFM) message and they must stimulate an emotional response. A well crafted story or a sharp picture that captures the essence of your customers' pain will have your prospects sold before they even have a chance to think about it.

In order to maximize the effectiveness of your visuals, choose words or images that have both dimension and movement. Video and photos of real human beings (or animals) tend to be more powerful than graphs or sketches and drawings. Research has shown that when presented with photos of people in danger or in pain, your old brain recognizes and responds much more quickly than if you were shown that same information in a cartoon, word, or graphic form.

Even though you may have mistakenly assumed that a graph is highly visual, 99% of them contain either too much information or too many numbers to be effective at producing a decision. They can easily have the undesired effect of causing your audience to feel the need to "think about it". Remember, your primary objective is to capture attention and trigger emotion swiftly. Wherever possible, you want to prevent your would-be customer from sending the information up to his new brain for thinking, processing, and long delays.

> **KEY POINT**
> **Not all visuals have the same impact. The most powerful ones will resemble real life and have both dimension and movement.**

Once she saw the writing on the wall, Tracy knew exactly what I was talking about and what she needed to do. After all, visual communication was her area of expertise. She had forgotten to paint a clear portrait and show her prospects how she could bring their brand to life and draw more customers in to their businesses.

She got to work and started rebuilding her website again, this time with a strong visual emphasis. She removed all unnecessary copy, references to why she started the business and how she got into graphic design, from the main pages of her site. In their place she showcased, front and center, her most potent and powerful work. The homepage featured a close-up of a woman picking at a small piece of food stuck between her front teeth. The simple claim underneath created an instant snapshot of how her work would captivate the attention of her clients' audience:

Once they see your brand and message, they'll be
hard pressed to think of anything else.

She also included a slideshow of her recent work for various satisfied clients, and video testimonials. Tracy's prospects got to see and hear from real business owners how she had helped them transform their message and boost their sales.

Essentially, Tracy let her work speak for itself. Instead of clicking away because the site was too wordy and hard to digest, her users stayed on average 2.7 minutes longer, viewed twice as many pages, and the requests for more information went up by 22%.

I spoke to Tracy recently and she was much more upbeat. She couldn't believe she had even considered trying to compete on price with the overseas suppliers. And she couldn't believe that she had been so stupid (her words, not mine) as to ignore her greatest asset—the power of a strong visual message to connect with and convince her customers.

If you are being honest with yourself right now, how visual are your marketing and sales assets? Have you loaded them up with words, graphics and stuff that only means something to you? Or have you been careful to paint a clear and simple picture in your prospect's mind—to trigger emotion and engage the decision making part of his brain? If you have used pictures or video, do they serve a purpose or are they just there to fill up space, show off your assets, or generate a laugh? Remember, visuals offer a valuable opportunity for you to connect with the primitive brain of your prospects without having to say a word.

It is worth noting that is also possible to paint a vivid picture with words—particularly if you are good at asking questions or telling stories. Wherever possible, ask questions that cause your prospect to have to build a picture or imagine a scenario in his mind's eye. When designing your next ad or sales message, ask yourself what questions you could ask right now that would move your audience into the use of your product or service. The sooner your buyer sees himself using your solution, the quicker he will "get it" and decide.

> **KEY POINT**
> Be very clear about the role of visual aids in your sales and marketing messages. They hold the power to convey and convince 40 times more quickly than anything you say or do.

Is Your Message Moving or Does It Make Your Prospects Move Away?

Old Brain Stimulus #7—Create Emotional Connections to Close More Business

After a shaky start, Eric and Helen had become two of the happiest business owners you could meet. They were, as the saying goes, "living the dream". Their lives were devoted to the running of their own small bookshop. They spent their days reading or talking reading, sourcing and selling good books, and generally pursuing a passion for all things literary. They counted themselves lucky to be able to spend their early retirement years doing something they loved, which also kept them vibrant and productive.

For all of that, the couple did have some growing concerns. "Our biggest worry is this computer-book thing," Eric told me. (At 65, Eric wasn't particularly comfortable with technical things so I knew he was referring jointly to online bookstores and e-books.) "If people can buy all their books without even leaving their homes, maybe they'll stop coming into our store?"

"It's not so much about the money," Helen went on, "though that does throw a wrench into our retirement plans, of course, but a big part of our joy from owning this bookshop is having the conversations we have with our customers. We'd hate for those to stop."

Eric vigorously nodded in agreement. It wasn't hard to see that the recent bankruptcies in the bookselling industry were weighing on his mind and heart heavily.

We sat silently for a few minutes, squashed into the small office at the back of the shop. I looked out the door toward the front, down the corridor of well-stocked timber bookshelves and past the small lounge area at the front in which Eric and Helen often held court. It was hard to imagine a bigger contrast between the experience of this setting and the experience of buying a book online.

"Do you remember what it was that brought you into this shop in the first place?" I asked. "Not as customers, but as owners."

"Well, there was a good business broker, I know that much," said Helen. "He convinced us we were getting a much better deal financially than we actually got."

"Yes," said Eric. "We were well and truly caught out there. It was partly our own fault though. We didn't make the effort to properly understand the business, especially the financials and the importance of cash flow, before we signed up."

"That's right," I said, "and there was a reason for that. You were both caught up with one of the most powerful stimuli that activate the decision making part of your brain: emotion. When this store became available and you had the means to invest, there was no stopping you. Any semblance of logical analysis or careful due diligence was pushed aside by your overwhelming emotional connection to both the shop and the idea of owning it."

The couple nodded in agreement. "You're quite right," Eric said. "I just couldn't help myself. I think, in retrospect, that I did have some concerns about the terms of the deal, but I got swept up in my emotions and the dream of owning our own business, and I simply ignored the issues and risks."

I went on to explain that what I thought Eric and Helen needed to do now was tap into the emotions of their customers. And what I meant by that was something more ecological than blatant manipulation or preying upon emotions for strategic advantage. In fact, there are many trainers and programs who advocate using neuro-linguistic programming (NLP) tactics to create a sense of artificial urgency or scarcity. What I was proposing was something quite different—building an authentic emotional connection so strong that, no matter how much the internet tempted, Eric and Helen's customers would keep coming back and recommending their products and services to others.

In many ways, you can think of emotion and repetition as the adhesives that cement events to your memory. As leading American neuroscientist Antonio Damasio puts it: "We are not thinking machines that feel, we are feeling machines that think." Emotions play a part in virtually every decision you make, whether you like it or not. When something has an emotional impact on you, you are more likely to remember and react; in that way, your strongest emotional responses will stay with you for your entire life because they created a deeper engram (or impression) on your mind.

> **KEY POINT**
> **The greater the emotional response triggered by your message,**
> **the more likely it will bond to your prospect's mind.**

Your emotions produce strong electrochemical responses that have been proven to directly influence the way you handle, respond to, and hold on to information. The cocktail of hormones that floods your mind when you experience strong emotions causes the connections in your brain to speed up, intensify, and be reinforced.

A strong emotional trigger is much more likely to drive you to buy a product than a rational argument for doing so. In fact, as Eric and Helen found out, an emotional impulse can often lead to purchasing something, despite strong logical reasons for *not* doing so.

Think about the books that stay with you long after you have finished them, or the movies or music that lives on in your mind long after the lights go up and the sound fades away. Think about the headlines, photographs, and stories that you know you will never forget: the assassination of President Kennedy, the 9/11 attacks, the first steps man took on the moon, or the death of Princess Diana. In each of these cases, the potency and vividness is directly correlated to the depth of your emotional response to the story, the images you saw, and the context.

Emotional connections occur because your feelings are stirred. This happens whenever you "put yourself into the situation". So a story becomes great or memorable when it hooks you in—it effectively makes you a part of the scene and you *feel* the feelings of the characters. That is why news of a missing infant has a particularly strong effect on you if you are a parent, because you can *feel* the angst and despair of the parents who may never see their child again.

> **KEY POINT**
> Ads that cause your customers to reconnect with or rediscover strong emotions from their past and associate those with your products or services, are more likely to trigger the part of the brain that decides.

As a buying stimulus, emotion is incredibly powerful. And there is no more effective way to tap into or unleash the emotions of your prospects than to tell them a story. Storytelling has the added bonus of fusing the decision making drivers of commonality, closure, visual cues, and emotion. Through the ages, we have passed on our history and our wisdom to our children in the form of stories. As a child, you likely came to expect a story from the people that you loved and looked up to—your parents, grandparents, older siblings, teachers, ministers, babysitters, and neighbors. Your brain felt comfortable and safe with both the stories and the storytellers.

That is why even now, as a fully grown adult, you are still susceptible and more likely to let your guard down when you hear a good story. You are so used to hearing stories from people that you trusted in your childhood, that you automatically let your guard down and are much more likely to take in the message at a deeper level in your mind.

In that same way, a persuasive advertising campaign will draw you in emotionally by compelling you to *feel* the pleasure or relief of using a product well before you own it. Some of the best examples of this in advertising have little or no content but are jam-packed full of emotional cues. Apple demonstrated this masterfully in their campaign to infiltrate your heart and mind with their iPad device. Despite the fact that it doesn't have a USB port, HDMI plug, or support Flash, Apple somehow managed to convince 15 million people to buy one in 2010. They captured 80% of the new tablet market and many of you are still on waiting lists in some countries, because the demand far outstripped the supply. After all, who can resist "having the whole world in your hands?"

I suspect that if you look back now at the six buying stimuli I've described earlier and the way they have been used by business owners just like you to create powerful messages, you'll notice that, deep down, emotion (and storytelling) was used strongly in each one of them. Think about the connection that Carol created with her client-centered message: any woman who has ever had or seen a bad haircut could identify with her ad immediately. Similarly, Sam identified and triggered the most feared outcome for any bride-to-be—wedding photos ruined by wet weather. And Charlie beautifully connected with the nostalgia that many of his adult customers felt when reflecting on crafts and hobbies they shared with their own fathers.

> **KEY POINT**
> To shorten the sales cycle and close more business, your message must allow patrons to *feel* the pleasure or relief of using your product or service long before they actually own it.

If your customers cannot remember your message, how can you reasonably expect them to choose you? What stories do your prospects and customers need to know right now about your product or service? What emotions (if any) are you triggering when they see or hear your materials? Or is it safe to say that you might just be putting them to sleep with too many big words and not enough feeling?

So what of Eric and Helen? After we talked about this a bit more it became clear that their most valuable emotional asset was the community they had created in their bookstore. There is nothing like a tightly bonded community to make you feel as if you belong, as if you "own" a part of the connection that exists between you and others. You and I feel a sense of comfort and support from our community which is second only to the bond we share with our family. In a time when "street level" unity is much weaker than it used to be, community is still the secret behind the success of Facebook and other social media tools—even if online bonds are seemingly less tangible and intimate.

Eric and Helen didn't have a lot of knowledge or interest in online communities, but they had a passionate interest in building a stronger local community of paperback and hardcover lovers.

They started by producing a newsletter (on paper) once a month, including reviews written by themselves and their regular customers. They initially distributed the newsletter inside the store and by letterbox drop in the local area. Over time, they also built up a sizeable and attentive mailing list. Pretty soon they began advertising regular events in the newsletter: guest speakers, book discussion groups, kids' events, and even the occasional book launch. All of these things got people to come into their local bookstore (frequency of visits was up almost 11%); as people came in more often, they got to know each other and built bonds based on common interests and favorite authors. Eventually a young man offered to create an interactive website for Eric and Helen, and to their surprise, they began to add more young professionals and teenagers to the mix as well.

Over time their community continued to grow, and while the rest of the book retailing world seemed to lurch from crisis to crisis around them, Eric and Helen just kept building stronger and stronger emotional connections and steady sales growth figures of 5–6%. While they may not be able to compete with Amazon based on selection or price, they were able to be everything that Amazon isn't and never will be—a great place to enjoy a cup of coffee, touch and feel the books before you buy them, special order what you want, and receive a recommendation from a trusted friend.

They're getting on a bit now, Eric and Helen, and one day I guess they'll have to retire properly. Believe me, that will be an emotional day for their customers.

KEY POINT
Emotion creates the movement that is required to drive your customers forward in the buying process.

PART TWO

7 Steps That Help Your Prospects to Say "Yes"

Most business owners and sales/marketing professionals make the fatal mistake of wasting 97% of their efforts on where to put their message, how much copy to use, and how prominently to feature their logo. As you now know, focusing on your promotional vehicle, your brand, and your features and benefits is of little or no use. They have no impact on the real decision maker of your prospect—the old (reptilian) brain.

An eloquent and logical message is often not enough—in order to be effective, the old brain needs to understand, remember, and feel compelled to act. No matter which medium (print, website, PowerPoint etc.) or which type of message (direct, mass, face-to-face) you use to promote your product or service, by following the 7 Step Sales Seduction Process you are guaranteed to make an impact on the decision making part of your prospect's brain.

The Sales Seduction Process will create a strong foundation for your campaign or message—these secrets will help you to craft campaigns that close more business. They have been carefully constructed to help you create a high impact, memorable, and compelling message.

Is Your Message Forgettable?

Step #1—Capture Attention

Ian looked at me with an apologetic smile.

"Do you mind?"

"Of course not, I'll be delighted," I laughed.

I was having coffee with Ian, a client I'd helped two years ago. With a little help from me he'd turned his faltering high street shoe shop around and was now busy enough to employ a manager, giving him time out for a leisurely chat over a cup of coffee.

Ian had asked me to see Bill, an old friend of his. Bill was depressed and feeling at a loss. After a long and successful career in pharmaceutical sales, things weren't going so well. In fact, they were disastrous.

When we met up the following day I was immediately struck by Bill's impeccable appearance. Dressed in a traditional dark blue blazer and crisp white shirt, with his tie perfectly knotted, he reminded me of an "old-school" headmaster. His wide blue eyes crinkled at the edges as he smiled in greeting.

"Thanks for this," he said, reaching for my extended hand and shaking it courteously. "Ian told me you were a straight shooter, and right now I need all the help I can get."

"I'm here to listen, Bill," I told him.

Stirring his tea methodically, Bill explained his predicament. He'd been with PharmCare for the last decade but prior to that had earned his sales stripes in a succession of pharmaceutical companies, rising steadily through the ranks and gaining a solid reputation for reliability. I could see he was quietly proud of his achievements and experience, considering them both essential sales tools. And clearly PharmCare respected his history of success, appointing him senior sales manager and trainer of a team of young go-getters.

"Apparently, over the years I've become a bit of a legend," Bill said, smiling shyly. "I tend to get a free hand most of the time. You know, I prefer to be out doing the real work instead of attending all those new product launch and R&D meetings. It gives me more time to call on my clients and make sure they're happy."

"Aren't those meetings a help for closing sales?" I asked.

"Well, sometimes, I guess," Bill said, thoughtfully. "But with the way sales are going, we should be spending more time calling on our clients than sitting around in meetings discussing which new products are best and how they were developed. Reviewing market feedback and scientific studies is all very well and good, but it's obvious that sales are down across the company and we are dealing with a much tougher, more competitive environment. Many of my customers are trying to source product direct and they are overwhelmed with requests for sales meetings with reps like me."

Bill shifted in his seat and sighed.

"And now my clients want to change everything."

"Change?" I prompted.

Bill looked at me glumly.

"You know it's really hard to win new clients these days, and that's something I used to be really good at. Until a few years ago it was so straightforward. I'd call on the prospect and introduce myself, making sure I left plenty of printed material about the company and our products. Then I'd follow up with regular visits for a coffee so the prospect could get to know me and my sales record. Later down the track we could really get down to the details over lunch."

"Didn't that take up a lot of your time?" I asked.

Bill grinned.

"For sure," he replied. "Sometimes it took months to reel them in. But once I had them, they weren't going anywhere, even when I changed companies."

His face fell again.

"Not anymore. It's almost as if they're avoiding me now."

"Give me an example, Bill."

Leaning forward, Bill looked at me anxiously.

"I've been doing business with Chris's pharmacy for over eight years. Chris wouldn't think of purchasing any stock without discussing it with me first and he's incredibly loyal. That's the sort of relationship we've had."

"Let me guess," I said. "There's a new pharmacist there now?"

Bill looked at me in disbelief.

"That's exactly it," he muttered. "Diane's there now. She's completely different. The way she's going about things—I don't understand how she's going to manage. Even though she knows my history with Chris and my position with PharmCare, I can't even get in to see her for 60 minutes. She's too busy with turning the place into some sort of Emporium."

I had a good idea where this was going. "Emporium?" I prompted.

"Hmm, I'm not sure I like it," Bill mused. "But I think I understand. As an independent, she's getting a lot of stiff competition from a new nationwide outfit just a few blocks away. She wants to clear a lot of established lines and expand her range to include more non-pharmaceutical products for young families. It's just the way she's doing it that doesn't make sense."

I nodded my encouragement.

"Go on."

Frowning, Bill scratched his head.

"It's like this—Diane has all the reps scheduled in for 15 minutes apiece. In that short time we're supposed to give a presentation and put whatever products we think will suit her on the table. She's told us she'll make her decisions there and then. I really like the lady, but it's crazy. Nobody can do it that way. Fifteen minutes isn't enough time to properly introduce myself, my company, and our history of successful products."

Bill groaned.

"It's not just about me," he said. "It's the people in my team. I'm responsible for their training, their careers, their success, their families—everything. I need to take care of them, and each one of them is expecting me to teach them my techniques of how to sell effectively."

Bill stared into his empty coffee cup.

"I know that I'm letting them down and I don't know what to do about it."

It didn't take long, after reviewing Bill's 15-minute presentation, to determine where he had gone wrong. Of the more than 27 slides Bill had carefully assembled, 17 were about him, his company, and their long history in the marketplace. He had so much background information to cover that he ran out of time to present his best products. But worst of all, he missed the crucial opportunity to capture her attention in the first 60 seconds.

Is it any wonder Diane didn't buy anything? Bill wasted his entire appointment on everything except for what Diane wanted and needed to hear.

> **KEY POINT**
> In order to be effective and make an impact, the old brain of your prospect needs to be awake and alert when you deliver your solution. That means, what you say FIRST must create an impression and captivate your prospect's interest.

The first and most important step in creating a sales or marketing message that closes more business is to become an expert at capturing attention up-front. If you are successful at quickly and strongly enchanting your prospect within the first 60 seconds, you stand a much greater chance of holding his interest until you can communicate your entire message.

As we discussed in Chapter 5, your brain is energy hungry. It is constantly looking for an opportunity to rest. Since the old brain is primarily concerned with your physical survival, it will operate at near maximum alertness at the beginning of every interaction you have with your prospects and customers. However, your level of attentiveness (and the attentiveness of your audience) drops down to as low as 20% in the middle. Essentially, once your prospect's old brain has scanned the environment and determined that it is safe to be with you, it powers down and tunes out. That is why your prospect will be most alert and will pay particular attention to the very first thing that you say or present to them.

Regardless of the length of your sales presentation or marketing message, you must capture attention and deliver your most powerful points up-front when your audience is most alert and receptive. Never begin by introducing your brand, building your credibility, talking about your competitors, or listing features and benefits. This strategy will put your customers to sleep and you risk having to deliver your most important claims and proof when your customers are least likely to remember them.

In order to capture the attention of your audience and hold it, you have to know the one (or two things) that are MOST important to them right now. This is something that you cannot afford to guess or assume.

Therefore, in order to make the greatest impact and charm the old brain of your customer, you need to do your homework up-front in Step #1 of the Sales Seduction Process. By taking the time to help your prospect understand, acknowledge, and quantify his pain, he will become clear about the true source and intensity of his pain, and you will reinforce (with his old brain) that it is safe to trust you and your proposed solution.

Chapter 8

KEY POINT
When you take the time up-front to understand fully, you earn the right to present your solution, and it is more likely to be accepted by your prospect's old brain as both relevant and appropriate.

And if you think about it, this is the exact same approach that our pharmacist Diane would apply in her own business. Customers approach her every day with health concerns and prescriptions. She doesn't blindly dispense medications without first consulting privately with each patient to ensure they don't have pre-existing conditions, allergies, or other medications which might cause a negative reaction. She also takes each patient carefully through the instructions of how to take the medication and which side-effects they need to watch out for.

And if you are being honest with yourself, how much more confident are you with your pharmacist when she follows this simple formula to ensure that she thoroughly understands your pain and specific situation BEFORE she dispenses the pills that will cure it? Would you still trust her if she gave you some blue liquid from an unmarked bottle behind the counter without even checking to confirm your details, your condition, your dosage, or your medical history?

Since the old brain is self-centered and concerned with its own survival, it is highly interested in alleviating any pain it is feeling. That is why your customers will spend more time, energy, and money trying to avoid pain (and trying to stay safe) than they will pursuing pleasure and comfort. What this means is that the old brain of your audience is primarily concerned with what they are losing, not what you might have to give them.

> **KEY POINT**
> In order to capture your audience's attention and earn the right to present your solution, you must first identify, quantify, and rank their sources of pain.

Let's walk through a simple process to do that effectively and review how Bill used it masterfully to understand what was important to Diane.

Before Bill could ever hope to seize and maintain Diane's undivided attention with a powerful opening statement or story, he first had to discover her pain. Pain can present itself in many different forms—in order to establish whether it is financial, personal, or strategic, you need to find a way to diagnose it accurately. For most business prospects financial pain will be the easiest for you to uncover and measure. Financial pain is about lack of results and most companies will measure how they are doing by a key performance indicator like gross profit margin, breakeven, cash gap,

Chapter 8

total sales, or return on equity (ROE). For a more detailed explanation or discussion of key performance indicators, you may want to refer to the Glossary of Financial Terms in *Financial Foreplay*.

Strategic pain is often more difficult to measure but it is just as significant and usually tied to the way that the organization goes about producing, distributing, and selling their products or services. To uncover strategic pain, you will want to explore business risk, quality issues, productivity, employee turnover, delivery challenges, supplier issues, market positioning, market share, branding, and other similar issues.

Personal pain may reveal itself to you as work/life imbalance, difficulty sleeping, strained relationships, excessive stress, indecisiveness, bad habits, and fear of moving forward. Anything that relates to the feelings and emotions that your prospect has around their financial or strategic issues, and resolving them, will fall under the heading of personal pain.

Thankfully, Bill had several hundred customers that he had dealt with over the years. It was easy for him to identify a good representative sample of 15–20 and to approach each of them with some simple questions to uncover the source of their pain and measure it. Even though these businesses were disparate in location, ownership, product mix, and competitive forces, 95% reported the same top two sources of pain: (1) decreasing or stagnant sales resulting in poor cash flow, and (2) declining market share. Curiously, 78% of them also reported similar personal aches such as stress, excessive work hours, and trouble sleeping.

Now we were getting somewhere. By asking some simple questions like, "What is the biggest challenge you are facing in your business?" and "When you think of buying a cold relief product for your shelves, what is the most difficult issue associated with acquiring it?", Bill was able to uncover a whole lot of pain. He now knew that his customers were struggling to maintain and grow their top line revenue. They all pretty much carried the same lines of product (both pharmaceutical and non-pharmaceutical) and it was getting more and more difficult for them to establish a point of difference—a reason why customers should shop with them and not with their competitors. He also discovered that many of them were carrying way too much stock in certain lines because they hoped the variety and choice would bring more customers in. Many of them were under pressure to rationalize stock and only carry items that were going to sell quickly.

This exercise was invaluable to Bill because he learned the most important lesson of all—his customers were in real pain due to the economic and competitive forces they were facing. They weren't interested in the products Bill had to sell; they were interested in finding the solution to solve their financial, strategic, and personal pain. Now all Bill had to do was find a way to determine which pain his customers were most likely to be motivated to alleviate.

> **KEY POINT**
> **Your prospects aren't interested in the products and services you sell; they are interested in finding the solution to solve their financial, strategic, and personal pain.**

The best part of all of this was that Bill was also able to establish that his customers were fully aware of their pain and able to tell him exactly what was giving them the most discomfort and concern. This point was crucial for Bill and is crucial for you too in conducting this same research with your own existing customers. In order to be most effective, your message has to address the specific pain that your audience has.

Similarly, all pain is not created equal. Do not waste your valuable time focusing on low intensity concerns. Generally speaking, the greater the pain, the greater the resources that will be employed by your customer to focus on the problem. This represents a fantastic opportunity for you to redirect that wasted time and money to buy your solution.

Practically speaking, it is easiest to work with pain that your audience readily acknowledges is severe and pressing. If a customer or prospect does

Chapter 8

not acknowledge their pain, it is impossible for you to provide the solution. However, if in their discussion with you they discover a new or unique pain that was previously unrecognized, give them time to properly digest and acknowledge it before making an assessment of whether it is intense or important.

Finally, you will need to establish whether your audience is motivated to alleviate the pain. Urgency is directly proportionate to the consequence that will be suffered if the pain is not cured. Your prospect will always be more likely to act if consequences are imminent or mounting each day. If there is not enough urgency around a particular pain, your prospect will tend to put off making a decision as his old brain is hardwired to focus on whatever is most critical to his survival right now.

In Bill's case, he was fortunate because the financial pain and pressure on Diane and his other customers was acute. They were highly motivated to fix the problem because many of them had cut their own monthly salaries to compensate for the drop in sales and cash flow. Out of the customers Bill spoke to, 13 out of 15 were also spending more than ten hours a day in their businesses, and it was taking a toll on them and their families.

Armed with this invaluable knowledge about his customers, Bill and I were able to finally sit down and plan his approach and next meeting with Diane. This time he needed to create the right first impression—to grab her attention up-front by letting her know that he understood her greatest source of pain. And if he was able to do this strongly, he would in fact earn the right to present his solution.

Given Bill's last encounter with Diane, he knew it wasn't going to be easy to get another meeting with her. He knew that he was going to have to do something distinctive and memorable.

I arrived at our next coaching session with a huge gift box. Inside of it Bill found a queen size pillow and a prescription pad sheet that I had mocked up on my computer for him. The prescription read:

NAME: Diane Mead

Rx: One good night's sleep. Repeats (10)

You'll sleep peacefully tonight knowing that your sales and cash flow have picked up by 12%. Give me 15 minutes on Monday the 14th and I'll show you how.

SIGNED: Dr. Bill

Bill delivered his parcel to Diane that same day. It probably won't surprise you to know that Diane contacted Bill later that same day to confirm their meeting for Monday and to say that she was looking forward to it.

This time Bill was prepared. He didn't bother with 27 PowerPoint slides and a long-winded introduction about himself, the brand, or his products. He went in with one simple slide that reinforced his message on the prescription pad, a handful of his best products, and some testimonials from other customers who had boosted their sales with those products.

Not surprisingly, Diane only allocated 15 minutes for their appointment. However, Bill was so successful at capturing and holding her attention that she ended up spending 50 minutes with him and she committed to buying seven new products that he suggested. She believed Bill when he said they would boost her sales and cash flow with one of her biggest customer segments—new and expecting mothers—because he proved it with evidence from other pharmacy owners.

As I'm sure you will agree, Bill's story is not really that different from your own. Every day you have opportunities to captivate and mesmerize your audience with your sales and marketing messages. But how many of these valuable chances do you waste by opening your presentation, email, or website with information that is all about YOU?

Shouldn't the very first thing that you say recreate or identify the primary pain that your prospect has? How much more effective would your materials

Chapter 8

be if your audience knew from the outset that you understood their primary source of pain and that you have THE solution that will cure it?

And there are many different techniques that you can use to capture the attention of the old (reptilian) brain of your audience. For those of you who meet face-to-face with your would-be customers, storytelling is one of the most effective methods. It draws upon all the principles that we talked about in Chapter 7, and it allows your prospect to put himself in the shoes of the person in your story. He will begin to see himself as being like the character in your story and you make it easier for him to imagine that he is actually experiencing the benefits of using your solution. Where possible use props, videos, music, and other tangible cues to draw your listener in and bring the story to life. If you are able to leave one of those with your prospect, you increase your chances exponentially of having him remember your message.

Some other great tactics that work really well in print and face-to-face are open ended questions, word plays, controversial statements, "before and after" photos, and unusual textures. Challenge yourself to present a simple, succinct message that engages the old brain of your audience and makes them beg to hear more.

And remember, before you can successfully devise a plan to achieve Step #1—Capture Attention, you need to first accurately diagnose the pain of your client. If you fail to diagnose the pain, it won't matter if you correctly master and use the 7 Stimuli That Charm the Old Brain.

KEY POINT
The very first thing that you say needs to recreate or identify the pain that your prospect has. When in doubt, allocate 70% of your time and effort to correctly diagnosing the pain and capturing the attention of your audience.

Which Do You Prefer—the Easy or the Hard Way?

CHAPTER 9

Step #2—Create a Clear Picture

When I saw Serena striding toward me, I was immediately struck by her chirpy confidence. I was pleased. She'd sounded upbeat on the phone, my first call from her since she'd revamped her business and supercharged her bottom line. This was purely a fun lunch date and I was looking forward to hearing all about her plans to expand from two locations to three.

"Hey, how are you?" she called out as we met just outside an upmarket, inner-city car dealership. In passing a few times, I'd noticed the place selling late-model secondhand cars and wondered how they could afford what had to be astronomical rent in this prime location. It wasn't just idle curiosity or the excellent cafe next door which prompted me to meet Serena here. I'd been keeping an eye on the business and had noticed the same high-quality, beautifully detailed vehicles sitting there week after week. I suspected the business wasn't doing too well.

As Serena and I hugged, I saw an attractive well-dressed young mother pushing a stroller and weaving decisively through the line-up of sparkling cars. Her eyes were constantly on the move, flicking from one vehicle to another, pausing here for a moment when something caught her eye and then moving on quickly. This was clearly a woman on a mission.

As I watched, a slim young man, maybe in his early thirties, dressed in a smart leather jacket and loosely tied necktie and with a welcoming smile already forming on his pleasant face, angled across the pavement to intercept his prospect. They would meet within earshot of us.

"Serena," I whispered, "this sales pitch could be very interesting. Let's see if this guy can give us some pointers."

She nodded eagerly and we eavesdropped on their conversation.

At first all seemed well. There appeared to be a natural chemistry between them—which perhaps was not surprising given they were both attractive, outgoing, and similar in age.

As he introduced himself as Tom and she as Sophie, I noticed that Tom seemed oblivious to her toddler in the stroller. The little fellow was waving his arms at Tom and doing his best to compete for the attention of his mother.

"What exactly are you looking for?" Tom asked.

"Oh, you know, something reliable," she replied glancing first at her little boy and then at a small yet sturdy SUV (four-wheel drive).

Tom thought for a moment and then his face lit up.

"I know," he said, turning to his left, "I'm about to reduce the price on this. It's my favorite and I've driven it myself. It doesn't miss a beat and it's still under warranty."

Tom began to walk toward a vibrant red 2-door coupe.

"He's lost it," I told Serena, who looked at me sharply, surprised by my comment.

"Lovely wheels though," Serena sighed. "If she doesn't, I will."

As Sophie followed Tom over to the sports car, I could see by the way she was still looking around the lot that she wasn't at all convinced this was the car for her.

"Look," Tom enthused, swinging open the driver's door. "Just eighteen months old and low mileage, this won't let you down. Isn't she a beauty?" And he spouted off a few impressive statistics about the car, which he thought would enhance the reliability in her eyes.

Sophie frowned.

"I was looking for something ..."

"Bigger, do you think?" Tom interrupted, striding back our way and then stopping at an impressive black 4-door sedan.

"Imagine driving this," he said with an infectious grin. As Sophie laughed and shook her head, Tom slid into the vehicle. With a soft hum the moon roof of the vehicle folded back gracefully, slipping neatly into a recess and disappearing.

"Heaps of room," Tom declared. "And just think, beautiful spring days are right around the corner. You can head off to the beach and enjoy the sun and wind on your face."

I could see Sophie's infant, confined to his stroller, becoming increasingly restless. She looked at him and then turned to Tom.

"Hey, thanks, you've been great but I need to feed and change my little man."

Tom looked shocked.

"But I haven't shown you everything yet," he protested.

"No, it's fine. I'll bring Jim, my husband, round on the weekend," Sophie said, beginning to move off and distance herself from him.

Tom shook his head.

"Well, thanks for calling round," he said, handing her his card. "Can I grab your phone number in case something comes in that might suit?"

"Best move yet," I whispered to Serena, as we watched Tom jotting the number down as Sophie left. "Come on," I said, taking Serena's arm. "Let's see if we can help Tom out with a few words of wisdom. He looks like the sort of guy that might be up for it? We may even help him save this sale too."

We found Tom at his desk quietly studying his shoes. He was deep in thought, with his back to us, and jumped slightly when I called out to ask if he had time for a chat.

Introducing ourselves, I quickly explained my work and told him that we'd overheard his conversation with Sophie. Tom wasn't in the least offended by my unconventional approach and seemed keen to talk about his lost sale. He also confirmed that things had been really slow at the dealership recently. In fact, the whole team had even taken a high-powered sales course but they hadn't yet realized any big jump in sales with all the fancy techniques they'd been taught.

"She seemed so right for one of the vehicles I showed her," he said about Sophie, unhappily. "And I was sure she was ready to buy today."

"She was," I agreed. "But you made it impossible for her to decide."

There is no shortage of formal training courses on selling. If you do a simple internet search, you'll probably discover over 100 programs that will claim to help you achieve or surpass your quota, close bigger deals, shorten the sales cycle, increase revenue, and make more money. And almost all of these programs will focus heavily on the component of rapport building.

Rapport involves getting in sync with and developing a relationship with your prospects. And as you discovered in Chapter 4, there is a very real, biological reason for doing this. The old (reptilian) brain of your prospect needs to feel safe and is hardwired to protect you—it will avoid anyone or anything that puts her in harm's way. To do business with your audience, you need to create or manufacture safety. Unfamiliar things represent a threat. That's why rapport building has received so much (perhaps even too much) emphasis in most sales training courses. The idea behind rapport is that your prospect is more likely to do business with someone she likes or who is like her.

For this reason, the majority of mainstream sales systems or programs will focus a significant amount of time and emphasis on rapport building in the first stage of approaching a potential customer. This means that you will likely be instructed to use a whole host of different techniques to help your prospect feel that you are on the same wavelength and understand them:

- Matching and mirroring (i.e. to adopt and direct the body language, gestures, vocabulary, and tonality of your audience)

- Learning to present your message in the representational style of your audience (i.e. visual, kinesthetic, auditory, and auditory-digital)

Chapter 9

- Using behavioral styles (i.e. DISC, Myers–Briggs etc.) to orchestrate what and how you communicate

- Breaking down your sales model into a series of sequential buying decisions where the customer is walked through information in a specific, pre-determined order

I have no doubt that these techniques are effective at assisting you to build rapport at an unconscious level and deliver your message in a language that is easier for your prospect's new brain (neocortex) to understand. However, in order to captivate the attention of and compel the old brain to react positively to your message and DECIDE, you must present your message in the language of the reptilian brain.

The disadvantage of these other new brain focused techniques is that you could easily get swept up and distracted by the process of rapport building. You could get lost in complex models and waste a lot of time trying to communicate in the "right way" information that is not even critical to the real decision maker (the old brain). While some of these techniques may work for some people, some of the time, they are not reliable or predictable because most of them ignore one simple fact—that the part of your customer's brain that decides is highly visual.

Neuroscientists estimate that approximately 90% of your brain activity (and the activity in your prospect's mind) is dedicated to processing and interpreting visual stimuli. While traditional sales training would have you believe that only 40% of your audience is visual, the truth is, the real decision maker is predominately visual.

Your retina captures images and sends that data on two distinct paths—one goes up to the neocortex and the other goes directly to the reptilian brain where it is processed and acted upon in only 1–2 milliseconds. Because your optic nerve is physically connected to your old brain, it is able to process visual cues 500 times faster than your neocortex and 40 times faster than auditory cues.

> **KEY POINT**
> Your eyes control your brain—and this is also true for your customers.
> That's how important visual cues are to your physical survival
> and to the effectiveness of your sales and marketing messages.

So where did Tom go wrong? He had taken a lot of sales training and had become quite proficient at assessing the representational and behavioral styles of his prospects. He knew how to put his prospects at ease—in fact, he demonstrated that by building rapport with Sophie, and by identifying that she was highly visual, people-oriented, and extroverted. Everything that he said and did in their short interaction together was carefully orchestrated to make her feel at ease and yet, she walked away. Even though her words and body language said she wanted to buy, Tom lost the sale because he made one fatal mistake—he spent all his time trying to persuade the wrong part of her brain.

> **KEY POINT**
> In order to compel your audience to say "Yes", you
> must present a clear visual representation up-front
> of how your solution can impact their world.

Now if you go back and carefully study the interaction between Tom and Sophie you will see that Tom spent a lot of time telling her what he thought she needed in the language he thought she needed to hear it in. Unfortunately, telling never leads to selling. As you can see, Tom skipped Step #1—Capture Attention. He jumped right into rapport building and presenting his features and benefits, which were next to useless in Sophie's mind. He never bothered to take the time up-front to understand, quantify, and rank her sources of pain. In fact, he only asked her one open ended question about what she needed. And even then, he jumped to a premature

Chapter 9

conclusion when he should have slowed down and taken the time to earn the right to present his solution.

Unfortunately, as amusing as this scenario might seem to you right now, it's not all that uncommon. It's happening right now in sales presentations, press releases, social media posts, and marketing brochures right around the country. And this rookie mistake is being made not just by small business owners but also by the senior marketing managers of large multinational companies. They (and you) have fallen into the trap of taking shortcuts and making assumptions about what customers want and need. And in doing so, you have done your prospects a huge disservice. You have deprived them of the opportunity to acquire the solution from you that would have cured their pain, because your message was confusing, overwhelming, or impossible to interpret.

That is why having a simple step-by-step process is so critical to getting your message right before you try to communicate it to your audience. It enables you to get crystal clear about the pain that your prospect is in so that you don't waste any of your (or her) valuable time communicating "fluff" that is not crucial to her decision making process. And it makes it so much easier for you to present up-front a clear picture of how your solution can impact and change the world of your prospect. Once you have captured the attention of your audience, your next step (Step #2 of the Sales Seduction Process) is to help her see how her life would be different with your solution.

So I bet you are wondering what happened with our young car salesman Tom? Thankfully, even though he blew his first encounter with Sophie, he was smart enough to get her number and he had time to prepare properly before his next meeting with her.

I quickly went over with Tom the key points that we covered in the last chapter about identifying, quantifying, and ranking pain. In about ten minutes we had mocked up five or six key questions that Tom needed to ask

Sophie so that he could fully understand her pain and begin to prepare for their next face-to-face meeting.

When I returned to the dealership the next day around noon, Tom ran out to the lot to greet me and regaled me with a summary of how his call to Sophie had unfolded. You see, Sophie was very clear about what she needed and what was important to her. This new vehicle was a replacement for the 2-door sports coupe that she had been driving since she first met her husband. She loved her car but it just wasn't practical and safe anymore now that she had her son. In fact, she'd been worried a lot lately about its reliability and the fact that it didn't have some of the newest safety features that would protect her child in the back seat in case of an accident. He also discovered that her back had been hurting her lately when she bent over to pick him up out of his car seat and put him into his pram. And finally, she confided that fuel economy was really important to her since she'd been on maternity leave and they'd been relying on one income.

Tom now had a very clear picture in his own mind of what was going to cure Sophie's pain. So much so that he wasn't even fazed when Sophie showed up again two days later with her husband and her child. Tom took his time and he captured her attention immediately when he let her know that he had done his research online and selected the vehicle that had the highest safety ratings for children and passengers. When he took her to the mid-size SUV, he first opened the back passenger door to reveal that he had already fitted it with an infant car seat and he helped her get her little man out of his pram and safely into his seat—all the while reminding her that this would be so much easier on her back since she didn't have to bend over to place him into the car seat.

Then he held the door for her so that she could climb into the driver's seat and see for herself what it would be like to operate the moon roof or adjust the seats. And just before he handed her the keys and sent the family off for a test drive, he let her know that there was plenty of fuel in the tank and that it got exceptional mileage since it was a hybrid. By the time Sophie and her family got back from their test drive they were already sold on the vehicle. Tom didn't need to present any other options or waste time talking about the features of the SUV. Tom had already done what he needed to do in order to help her make a decision—he'd allowed Sophie to step into and drive her solution. He showed her exactly what life would be like if she selected the solution to her pain of needing a safe, economical, and ergonomic vehicle.

I could see the pride and satisfaction on Tom's face as he recounted the story to me the next day. In Tom's own words "this was the easiest and most rewarding sale I've ever made. I knew exactly what she needed and it felt good knowing that I could just focus on her needs and not worry about complicated sales techniques and communication styles." This was a really vital point for Tom and for the entire sales team at the dealership.

It's very easy to get caught up in and waste time on techniques and semantics. But if you want to shorten your sales process, avoid requests to discount your price, and help your customers to remember, understand, and act on your message, you need to deliver a visual representation of how your solution will impact or change their world. If you fail to do it up-front (very early in the sales or marketing process), the decision making part of your prospect's brain will switch off and you will lose the sale.

When in doubt, use imagery, stories, and language that compel your audience to put themselves into the solution. Invite them to imagine or visualize the scenario. Show them a clear "before and after" shot or tell them a story about a customer who is just like them. Engage their imagination and their senses to test drive your solution right now. Make it easy for her to say "Yes" today.

KEY POINT
If you fail to deliver up-front a clear visual of how your solution will impact your prospect's world, you will likely lose the sale.

Do You Have a Problem?

Step #3—Confirm a Common Problem

As soon as I saw Natasha, I could tell something was troubling her. Although she smiled bravely, the worry lines on her face had deepened since our last meeting at a local business get-together less than 12 months ago. Back then she'd confessed to me her number one business concern—she was struggling to find enough money to advertise and promote her products properly.

Looking at her now, it was obvious to me that this issue with her marketing budget was still troubling her.

We went through to Natasha's office and as she busied herself making coffee, I thumbed through her latest catalogue and checked out some product samples lying on a nearby table. There was no doubting the quality and innovation in her collection. Everything was hand selected by her, beautifully crafted and in most cases, award winning. The colors and modern designs stood out, and in an industry dominated by cheap imports, Natasha's products were safe, reliable, and stylish.

Natasha's customers include the most exclusive boutiques and all of the national chains in the pregnancy and infant market. She has exclusive distribution agreements in place with her overseas suppliers which means she is able to bring in some of the most talked about new products in the international market—the only downside is that she must educate both the retailers and the customers about these new brands to create demand.

Most of the chains and multinationals want to offer her products at or near the recommended retail price of their overseas counterparts. This makes it difficult for Natasha to build in a bit of a buffer for marketing when she sets her prices. She has to be very clever in what she does to promote her products and she relies heavily on her good reputation in the industry and her strong relationship skills to open more doors.

Curious, I found my eyes gazing at a striking brochure with a large photo of a child sleeping peacefully and a device that looked something like an MP3 player.

"This is intriguing, Natasha," I commented.

"Isn't it?" she said over her shoulder. "The first samples came in three months ago and most of the retailers I spoke to had never heard of it but really like the concept. It's got two hundred lullabies featuring the hits from some of the world's best known artists pre-programmed into it. But the most impressive thing is, the musical arrangements are designed by child sleep specialists. They are orchestrated to gently encourage a natural, restorative sleep for little ones. Isn't it brilliant?"

"That'll fly off the shelves," I said, taking a seat at Natasha's coffee table.

"You'd think so, wouldn't you," she replied glumly, settling down opposite me with her coffee in hand.

I was surprised at her last comment. It seemed out of character. Her elfin features were seldom short of a genuine smile, and she was well known for her positive, direct approach. With the strong retail contacts she'd established over the last six years, everything should have been ticking over nicely.

I nodded at her to continue.

"This device and some of the other new items just aren't moving as well as I expected," she explained. "Retailers and customers aren't familiar with these brands even though they've received awards and publicity overseas. Many are reluctant to let go of the older, established lines and my competitors are discounting heavily to maintain shelf space and market share."

"What have you tried?" I asked.

"Well, many of my retail customers have asked me to pitch in and help create awareness and demand for these new products with media exposure. As you know, I don't have the budget for a full page spread in one of the popular parenting magazines, so I tried issuing some press releases to let the journalists and bloggers know about our exciting new products. I sent the press releases everywhere I could possibly think of—newspapers, radio stations, parenting forums, and TV stations."

"And?" I asked, knowing what her reply would be.

Natasha shrugged.

"Not a single bite. Not one person expressed interest. I followed up by phone and by email until I was blue in the face and I just kept getting nowhere. I really thought it would work, but it turned out to be a lot of effort for nothing."

"Not for nothing, Natasha," I consoled her. "At least you've discovered what NOT to do. What exactly did your press release say?"

Natasha paused and thought for a moment.

"It said that we're announcing our new spring line and that we've got a lovely new range of organic clothing, meal sets, an award winning feeding system, and a new post-natal support garment that's all the rage in London. That's about it basically."

My eyes went back to the brochure with the enchanting picture of the blissful, sleeping child.

"Oh, that," Natasha said, following my gaze. "That product is a bit difficult to explain in a press release. It's supposed to be quick and snappy ... isn't it?"

"It is," I agreed. "Short and memorable is the key. However, your press release has to have a point—a point that is relevant and of direct interest to the journalist or blogger who receives it. And the only point that matters to a media outlet is NEWS."

PR is a very different beast to mainstream advertising. Confusing the two is a common mistake that 99% of business owners unwittingly make.

When you take out an advertisement in a newspaper or online, you pay for the privilege to talk about your product or service. The media only cares about what you do when you pay them to be in their publication or on their show. If, on the other hand, you want them to give you FREE exposure, you need to either enhance what is going on in headline news or you need to make news of your own.

The media exists to report on the news and they are not in the business of selling your products or services. It is impossible to gain publicity by trying to sell your product or what you do to the media directly. Selling to the media will only guarantee that your press release or samples land up in the garbage bin along with the 10,000 other blatant sales pitches they received today.

The key to captivating their attention and winning free exposure is to make what you do relevant in the context of what is happening in the news. When you tie what you do to someone or something that is newsworthy, you make it easier for the blogger or journalist to do their job properly and you will stand out head and shoulders above the 99% of other businesses that sent their faxes and emails today. Helping to create or enhance the news is the quickest way to become the go-to expert in your niche for the top shows, magazines, websites, and newspapers.

In fact, journalists are the perfect example of Old Brain Stimulus #1—Is Your Message Self-Centered? The media is 100% focused on what is going to sell their program or publication today. In order to accomplish that, they are on the lookout right now for stories that relate to breaking news or celebrities. Why? Because the average listener or reader is obsessed with the news and with the lives of famous people.

In fact, the world's most successful news agencies thrive on the fact that you and I have a voracious appetite for news, sports, politics, and the private lives of celebrities. That's why on June 25, 2009, the number one news story for the day in almost every country in the world was the death of Michael Jackson. Even though there was major unrest in Cambodia, Thailand, Iran, and North Korea, a train wreck in Washington, and an announcement about the swine flu, Michael Jackson's death headlined and dominated the news for the next 48 hours. And if you had sent in a press release about your company, product, or service that week and it didn't have something to do with the Michael Jackson story, chances are you didn't get any coverage.

Chapter 10

The moral of this story is this—if you are newsworthy, you can exponentially increase your chances of receiving free coverage AND of having a sales or marketing message that stands out and compels people to take action.

So what's the easiest way to do that? The first way, of course, is to have a product or service that can add to, enhance, or present a new angle for a breaking news story. The second way to do it is to create news. Journalists care about problems that affect a large number of people. The larger the number, the more likely it will be relevant and interesting to their audience. Prospects and customers care about common problems too—the more common the problem, the more likely it is disturbing, worrying, and causing pain to your prospect right now. That's why if you want to create a message that captures attention and influences people to say "Yes" to what you do, you must complete Step #3 of the Sales Seduction Process—Confirm a Common Problem.

> **KEY POINT**
> **The more common the problem, the more likely it is to be disturbing, worrying, and causing pain to your prospective customers right now.**

In Chapter 4, you learned that we all like to do business with people we like, who are like us, and who want to help us. The part of your prospect's (or journalist's) brain that decides feels more comfortable with a familiar person or message. As humans, we like to know that the pressing problem we have right now with our marriage, our business, our weight, our pet, or the bug that's eating our tomato plant is shared by 72% of the population. We tend to take solace from the fact that we are not the only person who has this challenge or source of pain.

One of the best examples of this in recent history was a little advertising campaign known as "The Facts" in 2008 by GlaxoSmithKline, the maker of Valtrex (a herpes medication). Their scrolling underpants collage, featuring lacy thongs, striped bikinis, boxer shorts, men's traditional briefs, and even granny underwear, helped to strip back and dispel the myths surrounding who can contract herpes and how many people already have the disease. These stereotype-busting ads helped to educate us that one out of eight adults has herpes and that 80% of people who have the disease don't even know they're infected.

In this particular instance, the shocking combination of the statistics and the parade of all-too-familiar underwear styles, created a very strong impression in all our minds that this disease affects a large percentage of the population and it can happen to anyone. In fact, this campaign was so successful at creating awareness and drawing attention to The Facts website, it is still in circulation today. That's why it's absolutely critical for you to establish the commonality of the problem up-front in your sales, marketing, or PR message.

> **KEY POINT**
> Your prospect needs to know that he is not alone—
> that this problem he is experiencing is widespread and
> that you can help him to solve it once and for all.

And that's exactly where Natasha went wrong with her press release. In addition to a boring headline about her new spring line that probably caused 99.9% of recipients to delete it immediately, the body of her press release was really just a glorified laundry list of her new products. It had no point. There wasn't anything about it that was relevant, or newsworthy. It's no wonder that she didn't receive a single call or mention.

But the best part about this story is that all was not lost. The fact that she had been unsuccessful at getting media attention in the past had no bearing on what she could strive to achieve in the future with just a few small but important tweaks to her message.

Natasha and I spent two hours that day poring through the information she had on the infant lullaby device. What we discovered was that the manufacturer had already amassed some really good research that Natasha could use about infant sleep patterns and how the lack of regular sleep in the first six months affected the average family. Furthermore, we learned that a high profile couple—Elton John and David Furnish—had received it as a gift and raved about it to friends. We now had the building blocks to create a fascinating, relevant, and effective press release.

When I caught up with Natasha about two weeks later for our coaching session, she was all smiles. She'd just gotten off the phone with the leading pregnancy magazine in the country and they loved the information and the samples that she had sent them. Between the editorial mention they offered and the spreads she got in two national parenting magazines, Natasha estimated that she had easily gotten $25,000 in free exposure from just one simple press release and a handful of follow-up calls. Plus, she had been able to convince the editors to include the retail outlets that carried the product which would drive in-store traffic and benefit her customers.

Rather than bore the journalists with a summary of all the products that were new this season, we worked out a simple schedule where she could send out something new and enchanting to the media every other month. This allowed her to cover off each of her new products over time but focus each press release on the most newsworthy feature of each specific product.

Her first press release for the lullaby music device was a resounding success with the pregnancy and parenting magazines. It simply read:

Want to Know the Secret Elton John Uses to Get His Baby to Go to Sleep?

You are not alone if you are having difficulty getting your baby to sleep all night. About 25% of children under five struggle to fall asleep or refuse to go to bed.

And if your infant or toddler is not sleeping, it can disturb your own sleep patterns and make it more difficult for both parents to work.

*Want to know what celebrity parents like Elton John and
David Furnish use to help their little ones get to sleep and
stay asleep? Believe it or not, the secret is music ...*

And for those of you who have recently produced a media release, I highly recommend pulling it out now and reviewing it in light of what you just learned in this chapter. Pay particular attention to your headline. Does it grab the journalist's attention up-front with something that is newsworthy? Or is it all about you and largely forgettable?

Did you incorporate (or could you have) a real life story or some statistics to demonstrate to the reader that this problem (that you have the solution for) is real, pervasive, and universal? What are you going to do differently now that you know you need to establish that common problem up-front in order to get your share of media attention?

And remember, Step #3—Confirm a Common Problem applies to ALL your sales, PR, and marketing messages. It pays to focus on one product or service at a time. Wherever you can, try to make it easy for your audience to remember your key points—use an acronym like KISS (i.e. keep it simple stupid), a short phrase (i.e. stop, drop, and roll), a rhyme, or a mnemonic (i.e. contrast, concrete, commonality, closure etc.). These techniques charm the old brain and make it easier for your prospect to remember.

Neuroscience has also recently proven that your audience can only remember three to four pieces of related information for around 20 seconds before discarding them, unless a conscious effort is made to commit them to long-term memory via techniques such as repetition, word association etc. If you have a list of key points to communicate, try to keep it down to three or four so that your prospects or customers can take them in, recall what you have said, and decide to take action.

And some final tips ... Consider using research and statistics to demonstrate how common the problem really is. If you can, highlight the stories of well known people, companies, or organizations that had this exact same problem, and then reveal how it can be solved using your solution. Customers and journalists both love to know, with your assistance, how someone exactly like them or their readers overcame this widespread issue.

KEY POINT
If you try to emphasize everything, you end up emphasizing nothing. It is better to repeat your most important point for a second time than to introduce a fourth, fifth or sixth one.

Chapter 10

Have You Staked Your Claim?

Step #4—Construct Your Unique Claim

Does anyone really like going to the dentist? I bet it doesn't make your top three list of fun things to do today. And who can blame you for being a bit nervous when you think of your dentist in his clinical white jacket, snapping on his latex gloves, and easing you back in that monstrous reclining chair. Next, he shines that bright light down on you and you are left to wonder whether he intends to interrogate you for espionage or just examine your teeth.

Luckily, I was meeting my dentist Marcos under more civilized circumstances—a cup of coffee—and he was dressed inconspicuously in a smart casual shirt and dark jeans.

"It's difficult," he said, once we were settled in the lounge of his flagship practice, overlooking the bustling main city street. "As you know I have four practices here in the city. Each was strategically chosen to cater to the large number of surrounding businesses and office towers—so that our clients wouldn't have to walk more than a few blocks, struggle to find parking, or take public transport. You know, there are more than 1.2 million office workers within a five-kilometer radius of the city, so there is plenty of opportunity for us right here."

"And what sort of capacity are you running at?" I enquired.

Marcos's face dropped with disappointment.

"I estimate about 50%," he said. "Not quite enough to cover the rent and other fixed expenses. Raising prices again isn't an option either since our prices are already a bit higher than you'd pay out in the suburbs. I've got to find a way to bring in more patients so I can keep our dentists and hygienists busy."

"Do you get much walk by traffic?" I asked, gazing out at the solid flow of pedestrians streaming past us.

Marcos smiled and I could see how pleased he was that I'd asked.

"Yes, since we opened," he told me, "we've built a great loyal patient base and our regulars wouldn't dream of going anywhere else. In fact, if one of our existing clients transfers across town, he'll call us to find out where our nearest clinic is. We really provide the best dental care in the city, but we need more patients to discover how convenient and professional we are."

I suspected he was right about that. Marcos's business was first rate—his luxurious and inviting practice made the normally nerve-racking process of seeing a dentist more like a visit to a salon or a day spa. His offices were distinctly non-clinical, easy to get to and they delivered exceptional value for money.

"There seemed to be a high percentage of patients in your waiting area who look like they've just popped in from their place of work," I observed.

"You're spot on and I've done everything to attract that sort of clientele," he said, shaking his head. "I've offered corporate discounts, VIP specials, and late-night appointments. We've got a good solid base now but those old marketing strategies aren't bringing in new customers anymore and I'm starting to run out of good ideas."

"Has the state of the economy affected the frequency of your clients' visits?" I asked.

Marcos was emphatic. "Not at all," he said. "The demographic we attract are well paid, reasonably secure in their jobs, and they know the value of good dental hygiene and regular checkups. We just need to find more of them."

"What's the approximate amount of time one of your patients will spend in your clinic each year?" I asked.

Marcos didn't hesitate, he'd done his homework. "About two and a half days a year is the average amount of time," he told me.

His answer surprised me.

"So where are the 1.2 million office workers going for their dental care?" I asked, even though I was pretty sure of the answer. "And when?"

Marcos stared out the window at the crowd for a moment. "My best guess is that they take days off work. If someone with a 90-minute commute has an appointment at 11 near their home, why would they bother coming into work that day? Most will have sick leave, so it's easy to take the whole day even though they don't really need to."

"Hmm," I said. "So an office with 250 staff could lose around 625 days a year in productivity?"

"Well, I guess when you put it that way, you're right. It's a lot of wasted time!" Marcos exclaimed. "And some of that productivity could be saved if the employees came to see us. Most dental visits are preventative anyway but if we have to do some work—like a filling—the procedure is really quite quick and painless. We can have 85% of our patients back at their desks in less than one and a half hours. Our scheduling is so efficient that we rarely make a patient wait more than ten minutes and we provide a business center so that they can check their emails and make private calls if they need to stay connected to what's happening back at work."

Marcos thought for a moment. "But, as I told you, I've sent emails and brochures out to hundreds of surrounding businesses and we're just not getting many new customers these days. I need your help to figure out what to do."

Unfortunately, Marcos had fallen into the same trap that many business owners do. They send the same (or virtually identical) marketing messages out month after month and year after year. Even if the message is initially an effective one (which most are not), it can easily become irrelevant and lose its impact on prospects and customers.

As you now know, the key to creating campaigns that close more sales is correctly identifying, quantifying, prioritizing, and curing the pain of your prospects and delivering your solution in a language the reptilian brain can remember, understand, and act upon. Step #4—Construct Your Unique Claim is pivotal to your task of delivering your message to the old brain because it is precisely where you stake your claim, and your audience learns exactly what you stand for.

In order to illustrate why this is so essential, I want you to cast your mind back to the first few months after the global financial crisis of 2008. A lot of people lost their life savings during the stock market crash and many more lost their jobs. It was a horrific twelve months and few industries felt the shockwaves of the crash more so than the automotive sector. If you remember, new car sales dropped by almost 20% in a very short period of time and stayed that way for almost a year. That's a huge drop by anyone's standards and it devastated a key sector that is vital to the health of the national economy.

Despite the massive drop in sales across the board, one manufacturer actually managed to gain market share and outperform all other companies in sales growth that year. Do you remember who it was and why they were able to thrive?

Only one company stopped and took the time to identify, measure, and rank the pain their potential customers were in. They didn't do what all the others did—which was spend more money on newspaper ads, lay off salespeople, and slash new car prices.

Only one company assessed the change in the market, correctly diagnosed the pain, and came up with THE unique solution that solved that pain. *"If you lose your job and can't make your payments, we will take it back free of charge."*

Do you remember who that was?

That's right, it was Hyundai.

With one simple change to their focus, strategy, and message they stole market share from every other manufacturer. They were the only brand that correctly identified the shift in their customers' pain. They didn't keep pushing and reworking the same, tired old approach that clearly wasn't working. Yes, there had been a major downturn and the whole industry was hit hard, but there were still lots of customers who wanted to buy a new car but were concerned about job security and being able to make their payments.

And that is precisely why Step #4—Construct Your Unique Claim was so applicable to Marcos's message and equally pertinent to yours right now.

Chapter 11

Your unique claim is the reason WHY your audience should choose your solution. It should never be confused with "features and benefits". Features and benefits are data and information that explain your product or service, or what it does. A claim is something else entirely—it's your stake in the marketplace. Just as your ancestors may have staked claims to property, animals, or even minerals back in the day, your unique claim identifies to the world which territory you have marked out in your industry.

> ### KEY POINT
> **Your claim or claims are a succinct, clear, and tangible statement that lets everyone know what your core message is—the specific pain (or pains) that you provide THE solution for.**

To give you an example that fits in with our discussion about the automotive industry, when you think of the brand Volvo, what is the first thing that comes to your mind? If you are like 95% of people, you will likely say "safety". Isn't the running joke, *"It might look like a box with wheels, but it's still the safest vehicle on the planet."*?

Volvo doesn't claim to be the most luxurious, to have the best price, or provide the most exciting driving experience. They own "safety"—it's their primary claim and it's what they are known for worldwide. Volvo has owned that stake in the industry for decades, even though companies like Lexus, Mercedes, and BMW produce high quality vehicles that are arguably just as safe. We have been taught to associate Volvo with safety and no other brand has successfully attempted to challenge that claim. In fact, it is one of the strongest and most enduring claims in the industry. It addresses a key area of pain for many customers—especially the ones who worry when they transport their most precious cargo ... their children. If safety is the key area of pain for you when selecting your vehicle, chances are you either own a Volvo or are seriously considering buying one.

Essentially, if your claims are communicated effectively, they will naturally disqualify your competitors. That is why they are so powerful—you are teaching the old brain of your prospects that you offer THE only solution to their pain. Therefore, to help your audience take note and remember your claims you need to follow these important guidelines:

1. **Contrast**—The more contrast you demonstrate, the easier you make it for your prospects to decide now. Remember, you need to be the best in the world at what you do. Consider a claim to be the first, the biggest, the easiest, the most secure, the fastest, the strongest, the most convenient, or the most trusted etc. If you are not the best at what you do, you leave the door open for your competitor to come in and take the sale that should have been yours.

2. **Concrete**—In order to be understood, your message must be simple enough for a 6-year-old to understand.

3. **Repetition**—Repetition of your claims throughout your message sends a clear message to the old brain. It's like placing highlighting or a Post-it note on your claim which says "pay attention to this, it's important".

4. **Captivate**—Make it easy for your audience to remember your key points. Use an acronym like KISS, a catchy phrase, a rhyme, or a mnemonic (i.e. contrast, concrete, commonality, closure etc.). These techniques charm the old brain and make it easier for your prospect to remember. Wherever possible, limit yourself to a maximum of three claims. With the old brain, it is better to repeat and reinforce three claims than to introduce additional ones.

5. **Proof**—Provide concrete and tangible proof for each claim (more about this crucial point will be covered in the next chapter).

6. **Relevance**—Don't try to be all things to all people. If you are giving a presentation, do your homework beforehand to identify your prospect's pain and make sure your claim will solve it.

Chapter 11

KEY POINT
When communicated effectively, your claims will disqualify the
eligibility of your competitors. Your claims educate the old brain
of your prospects that you offer THE only solution to their pain.

So I bet by now you must be wondering what happened to Marcos and his budding dental practices? In order to get the most leverage for each marketing dollar, he really needed to reach large groups of employees within a few short blocks of his inner city practices. Therefore, his problem was somewhat unique in that he really had two distinct prospects—the first being the business owner (or HR manager) and the second being the employees.

Thankfully, Marcos was a quick study and he grasped the importance of doing his homework with both target audiences to identify, assess, and rank their pain. It only took him two and half weeks to speak to a good cross section of his existing customers and also a handful of HR managers in some corporations he wanted to do business with. What he learned from this process was priceless.

Not surprisingly the corporations hadn't really put much thought into where their employees were going for dental work. However, they were all very concerned about their productivity KPIs. In particular, they were interested in the statistic Marcos presented about the number of lost days due to sick leave taken for dental appointments. It was a huge amount of wasted time. In fact, most of the HR managers had incentives that were tied to minimizing sick leave and they were definitely motivated to find solutions to reduce it. They were also very impressed with his smartphone app and business center—they could see how it could help their employees to manage their time away from the office more efficiently.

The feedback from existing customers was slightly different. Eighty-nine percent reported the same top three sources of pain—uncertainty around the cost of treatment and coverage under healthcare, pain management, and the hassle of trying to schedule and get to appointments during the workday.

Interestingly, there was a common thread of pain for the business owners (or HR managers) and the employees around managing time economically. Both were keen to minimize the time spent travelling to and from dental appointments, but for slightly different reasons.

This provided an excellent opportunity for Marcos to stake a unique and powerful claim in his industry—*The Only Dentist Who Saves You Time and Money*. While other dentists in the area were all focusing on their expertise, their equipment, the atmosphere of their offices, and pain management, Marcos staked a strong claim that really resonated with potential customers and their employers. He also backed it up with solid proof (more about the various forms of proof and their impact on the reptilian brain in the next chapter). His short video email demonstrated the key points that backed up his claim—a map that showed how easy it was to get to the dentist, a demonstration of the smartphone app that would allow them to track their time, a tour of the business center, and a guarantee by Marcos that they would be in and out in under 80 minutes for 85% of procedures.

> **KEY POINT**
> When you make your claim, don't be clever or obtuse. If you have an important point to make be clear, short, sharp, and to the point. Your prospect needs to leave with a rock-solid understanding of the claims you have staked.

Notably, Marcos didn't bother to compete in a crowded marketplace with a copycat claim that was based on his assumption about what customers wanted. Therefore, he was able to get genuine traction with the employers that led to his message being endorsed by and promoted to large groups of employees.

In just under five months, Marcos's practices blossomed to around 69% of capacity. This 19% increase was crucial because it meant he was now turning a profit in each location and that he had more time and money to re-invest on growing his business and improving customer satisfaction. He was also able to get substantial testimonials from the business owners and HR managers that he had worked with, and these were very useful in opening doors with even larger businesses that Marcos had previously been afraid to approach.

And it doesn't matter whether you are selling dentistry, automobiles, or your product or service. Step #4—Construct Your Unique Claim is a fundamental building block that will ensure you stand out and influence more people. Remember, your customers are not thinking about you, your brand, or your features and benefits—they are thinking about their own survival and whether or not you can cure their pain. If you are able to stake a claim that is unique, memorable, and relevant, you will trigger the part of your prospect's brain that makes decisions and you will stand apart from all others. That's the power of Sales Seduction.

And if you ever wondered whether today is the best day to start re-examining and rebuilding your sales or marketing message from the ground up, then take a look around you. Businesses are closing their doors every day—which means more potential customers for the owners and managers like you that do survive. And in times like these, it's going to take more than just "doing what you and everyone else have always done" to secure the survival of your business and your livelihood. Uncertain times call for better questions, better decisions, and better strategies. In order to recession proof your business you need to shift your thinking around the way you do business and start providing THE solution (via a strong, distinctive claim) to the number one pain or challenge that your customers have.

KEY POINT
Limit yourself to a maximum of three claims. With the old brain, it is better to repeat and reinforce three powerful claims, than to introduce additional ones that might cloud the mind and delay a decision.

Have You Done Everything Except for What Your Customer Needs Most?

CHAPTER

12

Step #5—Cure Pain

I'd met Blaire the previous year at a furniture and accessories trade show. Pausing to take in the striking visual appeal of her booth, we soon found ourselves chatting. As we talked about the latest trends in home decor, I remember being unable to stop my eyes from perusing her dramatic display of eclectic furnishings and appreciating how outstanding her merchandising efforts were.

Getting together recently, she confessed sales were extremely sluggish across the board. Tearing my eyes away from a striking bedroom display that Blaire was fine-tuning, I turned to her.

"What do you attribute that to?" I asked, somewhat surprised. "You've got incredibly diverse and exclusive products and you've got a solid track record with your loyal customers."

I looked at her standing in the center of her makeshift wonderland. Blaire was dressed immaculately, despite spending most of her day hauling heavy items around and speaking to hundreds of prospects. She was as fit as a fiddle—it was hard to believe that she turned 50 recently.

"Well, I'm not entirely sure," she replied, turning her mouth down slightly. "I'm getting great exposure at these trade shows, but I'm not seeing many large orders from new customers. I'm still getting most of my sales from existing customers and our sales team has to work really hard and call in on them constantly to keep our orders up. We send out great emails each month packed with new merchandise but everyone tends to wait until the trade show or a visit from one of my sales team to place a big order."

"And why do you suspect that is?" I queried.

Blaire sat down on a nearby canopy bed and began smoothing away an imaginary crease on its vibrant silk duvet cover.

"Well, I don't really know," she replied thoughtfully. "Although things are a bit slow at the moment, I would have expected more orders than I'm getting each month. I think we provide fantastic value for money and I always try to include some amazing offers."

I looked at her quizzically. I knew her customers weren't mainstream or multi-store outlets. The boutiques that carried her merchandise were the sort of places you would shop at if you wanted a one-of-a-kind or exclusive imported piece.

"Like?"

Blaire shrugged as she searched the recesses of her mind for a good example.

"Oh, our last email announced a special shipment we brought in from Africa with some incredible handcrafted pieces and a few vintage items that I suspected would get snapped up quickly by the designers on our database. It looked great—we featured a large photo and blurb on each piece and some great specials (up to 20% off) on some of the items that were limited stock. Yet somehow we only managed to get about $8000 in orders which was well short of my expectation."

"So it's not about price then?" I queried.

Blaire had a puzzled look on her face.

"Well, it must be, surely, otherwise they'd be buying? And I can't afford to lower my prices any more," Blaire exclaimed.

"What do the retailers say when your sales representatives follow up these emails?"

Blaire looked a little embarrassed. Suddenly, there were a lot more creases to smooth out on her lavish bed linens.

"Actually," she said quietly, "most of them loved the new line and wished they were in a position to take up our offer."

"And?" I probed gently.

Blaire sighed.

"They were really apologetic. They said they'd love to order several pieces, but they couldn't even think about it until they got more people through the door. They were solely focused on bringing more shoppers into their stores by blowing out old sale items at 50% off."

"Knowing that, are you really surprised they weren't motivated by your message?" I asked, trying not to smile.

"At the time, yes, I was surprised," she replied even though I could see that her mind was racing to grasp the point I was making. "I couldn't understand why they didn't see the value in what I offered and I racked my brain to figure out what else I could do to get through to them with my message. But now I see things a lot more clearly. My customers weren't concerned about new stock or margins—they had bigger fish to fry. They just needed to find an effective way to bring in more traffic and I can't really help them with that."

"That's only partially true. Let's look at this with fresh eyes," I said. "Your customers like your products, but they need more shoppers in their stores to buy them, right?"

Blaire looked at me as if I were a bit silly and then nodded.

"So, if you can help your retailers to get shoppers in-store and spending money on home furnishings, that would be a good thing, right?"

Blaire's eyes were like saucers. She must have thought I was completely losing my mind.

"And how can I possibly do that?" she asked. "I think we already established that I'm not exactly a whiz at marketing communications."

I laughed.

"By leveraging your greatest skill," I said, gesturing around the impeccable trade show display. "And by proving to them that you have the solution that solves their number one problem."

Unfortunately, it's not enough to diagnose the pain of your audience and present your unique claims as THE best cure—you have to prove it to him. If the reptilian brain of your prospect doesn't believe that it will work, he simply won't buy from you. It's not enough to list your benefits or talk about your value proposition. To trigger a decision, you must prove that it will cure the pain. And to prove it to his old brain, you are going to need a lot more than a cost benefit analysis, discounts, pretty pictures, or appealing to common sense. The reptilian brain controls your survival mechanism—it is hardwired to be resistant to adopting new ideas, products, and behaviors. In your prospect's mind, change equals pain or danger.

The old brain needs to see a tangible gain and hard evidence from your solution. If the reptilian brain can see a concrete gain to his most pressing source of pain, he will decide. You must prove to him that the value to be gained by your solution clearly outweighs the cost. Sometimes that gain may be tangible and measurable and other times it may be related to benefits that are intangible, strategic, or personal in nature. When the gain is intangible and more difficult to measure (relative to the cost of your solution which likely has a dollar figure attached to it), you will need to work harder to prove to his old brain that the net gain is real and significant.

That is why you cannot simply stop at Step #4 in the Sales Seduction Process. Ninety-five percent of you have made the fatal mistake of outlining your claims and assuming that your audience should take your word for it. If you don't believe me, take out a copy of your last marketing piece (or refer to the homepage of your website) and confirm for yourself whether you made your unique claim or claims, and then proceeded to prove them beyond a shadow of a doubt. Chances are you didn't—not because you didn't have proof but because you assumed that you didn't need to bother. That one simple mistake, which had gone unnoticed by you until now, has cost you thousands in lost sales.

Step #5 in the Sales Seduction Process—Cure Pain is critical to your success in creating a campaign that closes more business, and to do it successfully

Chapter 12

you need to understand how the old brain views different forms of proof. Not surprisingly, all proof is not created equal.

> **KEY POINT**
> Your claims, or the value proposition of your solution,
> is not enough. You need to prove that your solution will
> produce a net gain for your prospect and solve his pain.

So let's talk now about the different forms of proof and how effective they are. I want you to imagine for a moment that you are a home decor retailer and that you are struggling to get foot traffic into your business and money in your cash register. Yes, I am asking you to step into the shoes of one of Blaire's prospects. And I want you to assume for a moment that she did not send you a pathetic email about her new spring line and a 20% discount on some limited availability pieces. What she sent you was something quite intriguing and valuable—a unique claim and an offer to cure your most pressing form of financial pain.

Now if she were to present this claim to you right now, which do you think would be more convincing to your old brain?

- Her dream or vision of how well it could work

- Statistics, numbers or graphs

- A trial offer for you

- A visual snapshot or story

- A customer testimonial

Let's have a look at each of these in turn and assess their potential to help you make a decision to buy from her.

What if Blaire were to approach you today (either by phone or by email) to talk about an idea she had to re-merchandise the front window in your store. If you spend $4000 with her on product this week, she will send her best person to completely redesign your window so that more of the foot traffic walking by every day will be enticed to walk through your door and actually buy something. But it is all just a concept in her mind (a vision of what is possible) and she is unable to show you exactly what it might look like or provide any evidence it will work. How persuaded would you really be to part with $4000 of your hard earned funds?

Without any tangible way to demonstrate the gain, Blaire is selling her vision and she is essentially asking you to act on blind faith, isn't she? Her idea, concept, or vision of how it could be if you bought her solution is going to have to be pretty irresistible and intense to get you over the line. And that is exactly why it is the least persuasive form of proof. Now don't get me wrong, it can be done and there are numerous examples of visionaries who do it very well. But unless you are Walt Disney, Sir Richard Branson, or Steve Jobs, you are going to struggle to muster the charisma and influence to pull off this form of proof in isolation. In most circumstances, if this is your only form of proof, you will lose far more sales than you close.

So let's try another approach. Would you be a bit more convinced if Blaire claimed she was the most sought after window merchandiser in the industry and she stated that "retailers with strong window displays get twice as many shoppers in-store and 23% more sales"? Based on what you learned about how the old brain decides in Part 1 of this book, this approach has one advantage and two disadvantages, doesn't it? On the plus side, she has quantified the upside amount for you so it is fairly concrete and tangible. Unfortunately, you know that the reptilian brain prefers visual cues to numbers and when presented with data, it will naturally kick the information up to the new brain for processing and analysis. In fact, your new brain is already wondering where she got her statistics, how reliable they are, and what an extra 23% would mean to you in dollars.

This attempt at proving her claim is not a total failure and she may eventually win you over. However, all things being equal, she has made the rookie mistake of triggering your new brain, which will at the very least delay your decision and put the sale at risk. Numbers, statistics, and graphs can be used effectively to prove your claim but this strategy should be used sparingly and with caution. If you must use it, keep your figures to a minimum and break the gain down to a very simple digit that means something to your prospect. If they measure a financial cost in employee hours, transactions per day, lost days per month, or dollars per transaction, make sure you present your net gain in their terminology.

Another possible way that Blaire could try to prove her claim would be to offer you a trial of her services. Imagine for a moment that she offered to come out and do a quick consultation at your store—or she offered for you to come into her showroom to view her existing displays. Would that sway your mind and get you over the line to invest $4000? If you are like most prospects, it just might. A demonstration of her solution or a trial will in most cases appeal to your old brain. You get to see, touch, or feel the product or service in action, and it allows you to step into the shoes of someone who has already decided. Your reptilian brain likes to try before you buy because it gives concrete evidence, closure (a "before and after" snapshot), and a very clear picture of what it looks and feels like to test drive the solution. If she is careful to construct an experience that touches on all four of these old brain stimuli, her message will likely charm you into a purchase.

The final two forms of proof are closely linked but differ somewhat in their impact on the old brain. What if Blaire were to send you an email with a humorous and endearing story about a little girl with long, golden curly hair who was wandering the streets in search of the best place to buy her furniture? She went from bland window to bland window until she found the one that was "just right" ... and lo and behold that store was full of customers because it had been professionally merchandised by the most sought after team in the industry. And, of course, you learned that you too could have a store full of customers and more sales if you called Blaire right now to book your window transformation before the holiday season.

Would this tale seem familiar and safe to you? Would it make you smile and be more receptive to her marketing message? Might you be tempted to give it a go based on the strong visual cues and the emotional connection you felt to the character who reminds you of Goldilocks? Chances are, you absolutely would feel drawn. This form of proof also touches on at least four of the key brain stimuli and as such, it is very convincing to the old brain. The stronger the visual cues and the emotional elements, the more influential your snapshot, metaphor, or story will be with your prospects.

But when it comes to proof, the most believable and credible by far is always a customer testimonial. Why is that? In addition to the old brain stimuli triggered by the trial and the story, the customer testimonial nails two more crucial elements—it provides evidence of contrast (between where the prospect is and where they want to be) and it is directly relevant. If the solution that Blaire is about to provide to you helped another retailer (that is exactly like you) to close $41,244 more in sales last month, you are highly likely to take her up on the offer immediately. As long as you see or hear the customer tell you the result he got with Blaire's solution, your brain will value this form of proof above all others. Remember, if Blaire tells you, it means one thing, but if the customer tells you himself—either by video or in writing—it means everything to your old brain. Social reinforcement is powerful and persuasive. If you hear that others like you have already gained from using the solution, you are much more likely to view and accept the solution as being ideal to cure your own pain.

KEY POINT
Your proof of gain must be delivered in a
manner that cannot be disputed.

Chapter 12

And that is exactly why Blaire chose to use a customer testimonial and a photo to back up her claim to be the most sought after merchandiser in the industry. Rather than focusing on the items she had to sell or her prices, her strongest claim became the fact that she provided the solution to her prospect's traffic and sales problem. Her proof, as featured prominently at the top of the email, was very simple and compelling. Blaire's message included a heading, a strong visual of the re-merchandised window, a convincing testimonial (complete with name, business, and suburb), and a call to action.

Want to Know How ABC Retailer Made an Extra $41,244 in Sales Last Month?
<photo>

"I was skeptical at first. Walk by traffic was down and I tried everything—sales and advertising—to get more shoppers in my store. The transformation of our front window was incredible. Having a strong drawing card has made a huge difference to our business this month. Sales were up by $41,244 and I will be using Blaire's team again next month to give us a much needed lift."

Brenda McCay, ABC Retailer, High Street

We are the industry experts in visual merchandising. For each $4000 investment in product, we will transform your front window into a customer and sales magnet.

Eight clients took Blaire up on her offer the first week she sent it out. That meant an extra $32,000 in sales and some additional upsells and top-ups because customers were buying the items right out of the shop windows. Blaire now gets regular requests to repeat this offer and she is even thinking of introducing a special VIP package where her best customers receive a window makeover each month based on a minimum monthly spend. Her customers love it because they get assistance to keep the shop looking fabulous, and Blaire's sales team love it because they now have more consistent contact and credibility with their key customers. All in all, it's a positive result for everyone.

So how can you take this information and apply it to your message and your audience? First, it is important to remember that you must demonstrate net gain for each claim that you make. If you have three claims, you will need to provide evidence of a tangible, intangible, and/or personal gain for each claim. It is possible to have more than one type of gain for each claim. However, for maximum influence, it is ideal to have at least one tangible or measurable gain for each claim. If this is not possible for a particular claim, it is a very good idea to use more than one intangible or personal gain to prove your point.

To evidence each gain, you have a host of available options. The most persuasive is always a customer testimonial. The rest (see bullet point listing above) range in order of effectiveness from least to most compelling. If your claim cures the number one pain of your customer, make sure that you include a customer testimonial in your choices of substantiation. You will want to guarantee that this vital claim and gain are accepted as fact by the old brain of your prospect.

I'd also like to encourage you to use a simple spreadsheet to outline and summarize your claims, gains, and proof. This approach has many clear benefits. It will help you to visualize where you have sufficient coverage for each of your claims and it will make it easier to identify obvious gaps or duplication. By writing everything down in point form, it will clarify your message in your own mind and it will ensure that every point gets remembered and translated into your final sales or marketing message.

And remember, what really counts in your message is curing your audience's pain and proving that your solution can do that. Before you say anything, ask yourself if you are training them on your product or service, or how it compares to the competition—or are you showing them something that

Chapter 12

will appeal to and trigger their old brain? If the information that you are about to share with your audience will not help them make a faster decision, omit it. More of the "same old same old" is not going to differentiate you from the pack, build trust, win customers, and grow your business. Take some time today to really think about what you have to offer and how it could be tweaked, improved, or redeployed to cure the primary pain of your customers.

At the end of the day, price is never really the determining factor. Once you uncover the true cost of the pain your prospect is in, price becomes irrelevant. Your customers will always be willing to pay a fair price for THE solution to their pain. Be unique—listen to what they need and be willing to do whatever it takes to deliver it. Anything less is simply a waste of your time and money on everything that doesn't really matter to your customer.

KEY POINT
There are several options that you can use to evidence each gain. The most persuasive is always a customer testimonial. The rest—your vision, numbers and statistics, a trial offer, or a visual snapshot—range, in order of effectiveness, from least to most compelling.

Why Does Your Prospect Look So Concerned?

Step #6—Overcome Concerns

Alicia is one of the most tech-savvy people I know.

She was in corporate IT for many years and is now out on her own, running a company that supplies online software to business owners by monthly subscription. I was keen to know how she was doing in her new venture. Alicia had made the jump to becoming an entrepreneur ten months ago so she could spend more time during the day with her two young daughters and work more in the evenings—a lifestyle she preferred.

Proudly showing me her studio—a comfy, warmly decked out loft, not the hardwired, high-tech, densely-packed cubicle arrangement I expected—she sensed my surprise.

"It doesn't have to look like a boring corporate office," she explained, setting two cups under the espresso machine. "Not anymore. Technology moves so quickly and the equipment I need to do this sort of work is smaller, lighter, and more convenient than what we worked on when I was coding high security banking software. Most of our projects are mobile applications so we spend a lot of time on handheld devices. It's liberating."

I nodded my approval. It was an inviting and funky workplace, very informal, with large couches and convenient coffee tables—perfect for meetings with tablets and other Wi-Fi devices.

"And how's your website?" I asked.

I knew Alicia's software was designed to help business owners monitor and maximize their return on social media. Her idea was to provide a one-stop application that would help them create and syndicate campaigns quickly across multiple social platforms—Google+, Facebook, Twitter, LinkedIn, YouTube, Pinterest, and their blogs. Her app also gave them access to practical marketing reports, video coaching, forums, and a full range of DIY tutorials. She was the first in her industry to offer a software as a service (SaaS) model where her customers paid a low monthly fee to access everything rather than a large up-front payment for set-up, licensing, software upgrades, and account management. It was an attractive offer for small to mid size businesses.

"That's an interesting question," she said, flipping over the bright yellow cover on her iPad as we relaxed back on one of the couches with our coffees in hand. "Here are some stats," she continued. "My unique visitor numbers are at 271,498 a month, up 20% from last month, and our prospects are spending on average 3.2 minutes on the site. It's the number of conversions that disappoints me. For such a great product, the results are really pathetic."

"Let's look at your site from the perspective of your customer," I suggested. "Perhaps you made it a little too hard for her to buy from you?"

Alicia looked puzzled as she navigated to her homepage and then handed me her iPad. I studied it for a minute and then asked, "What car do you drive?"

Alicia laughed. "I just bought a Mini Cooper two months ago. I've always wanted one. Why do you ask?"

"So you've never owned one before?"

"No, didn't I just say that?" she replied, looking at me oddly.

"Then how did you know that you'd like it?" I asked.

"Well, I took it for a test drive of course and I had a friend, who is a mechanic, have a quick look at it too. I wouldn't buy any car unless I'd driven it around for at least 20 minutes and it checked out okay."

"And why is that?" I asked.

"Well," she replied a bit abruptly, "isn't that obvious? Apart from wanting to know if I liked it as much as I thought I would, I had to determine if it was right for me and worth what he was asking for it. After all, it is pretty compact and I wanted to make sure it felt safe."

I stared at Alicia in silence, quietly smiling and waiting as her expression gradually turned from complete bewilderment to revelation and then finally, understanding.

"I guess that's where the expression 'try it before you buy it' comes from!" she exclaimed. "That's your point, isn't it?"

Now contrary to what you might be thinking right now, this isn't another story about proving your claim or gain. We just covered that in the last chapter. The point that I made to her and am now sharing with you is this— it's not enough to make your claim and prove to your prospect that she will gain from choosing your solution. You must also remove ALL impediments to her saying "Yes" right now. In fact, if what you do or offer is something that is new or unknown to your audience, you will have to work even harder to overcome the objections and concerns of the old brain and step them into your solution immediately. Anything less is guaranteed to drag out the entire process and cost you time and money. Step #6 of the Sales Seduction Process is all about just that—overcoming concerns.

As you know, the old brain of your prospect is hardwired to keep her safe. Take Alicia's web traffic, for example. The old part of the brain isn't going to decide anything if the new brain is full of questions like:

- Is this going to be easy to use?

- What if I don't like it?

- Will I be able to read the reports?

- How hard is it going to be to quit and stop the monthly payments?

- What if I don't see a benefit?

Now you might be thinking, *"But $49 a month is not a huge investment compared to the purchase of a motor vehicle."* And you'd be correct in your deduction—it isn't. But there is only one small problem with your conclusion. Your old brain isn't primarily focused on the magnitude of the numbers involved. It is fixated on keeping you safe and alive.

If the reptilian brain of Alicia's prospect perceives roadblocks and impediments to deciding right now, it will defer and kick the information up to the new brain for examination and further investigation. It's at that point that the new brain might start to think about the numbers and weigh up the relative risks of her specific offer. But, unfortunately, the damage has already been done—the decision has just been put off indefinitely and Alicia just lost another prospect after 3.2 minutes on her site. To put this into perspective, she was losing 99.5% of her audience every day, due in large part to the fact she forgot to remove all of the impediments to them saying "Yes" without delay. That is a lot of wasted money on search engine optimization, pay-per-click advertising, and promotion to drag traffic onto the site, only to see them disappear without a trace.

> **KEY POINT**
> If the old brain perceives obstructions to deciding right now, it will defer and kick the information up to the new brain for more thought and analysis. To close the sale now, you must remove all impediments.

And if you think about your own website or the last email you sent out, how many more customers could you have taken over the line if only you'd been more effective at drawing out their concerns and objections, and eliminating them? There is no point spending more money on marketing and sales if a large percentage of your audience is slipping right through your fingers.

Success at Step #6—Overcome Concerns comes down to your ability to draw out, or anticipate with certainty, the key objections or concerns. You need to do your homework up-front and dig deep by asking your customers and potential customers some crucial questions:

- When you think of acquiring X, what is the most painful issue associated with acquiring it?

- What worries you about making your decision to buy?

- Is there anything that would make it easier for you to say "Yes" right now?

- Is there anything that would cause you to think twice or walk away?

In sales and marketing, your strongest asset is your ability to ask the right questions. Questions really hold the answers to most of the shortcomings and rejections you've experienced to date. Particularly at this stage in the Sales Seduction Process, the right questions will deliver the answers you need to maximize your conversions and make it harder for prospects to think themselves out of the sale.

Success also comes down to your capacity to help your prospects put themselves into the shoes of a customer who has already purchased. Questions really are your most valuable asset. Instead of asking her something it is easy to say "No" to, ask her to imagine herself using your solution to save two hours a day per employee. Invite her to dream about what she will do with the $500 a week she just saved. Give her an opportunity to share with you the most important thing she will take away from your meeting and use. Or tempt her to celebrate the fact she won't lose any more sleep worrying about that old problem.

> **KEY POINT**
> To close more sales you must draw out the key objections or concerns ahead of time and ensure you eliminate them with your message.

Alicia learned a very valuable lesson that day. The answer to the problem of low conversions wasn't throwing more money at marketing efforts or ignoring it. She already had a decent number of leads, she just wasn't closing enough of them. When she took the time to speak with her existing customers and some of her prospects on her database, she learned some really valuable insights that transformed her website and her results.

Not surprisingly, almost every person she spoke to was suspicious about paying for a solution that they hadn't seen in action or heard much about. Most of them searched online for videos, social media posts, customer feedback, and reviews to find answers to questions like "How quickly will I see results?" and "Is it easy to cancel?" and "Can I use this software myself or do I need to hire another person to manage it?"

The solution for Alicia really came down to a couple of important changes to her strategy for converting browsers into buyers. In addition to the obvious additions to her website like customer testimonials, video demonstrations, and frequently asked questions, Alicia had to change her thinking and her process around sign-ups. The free trial concept was a tough one for her to get her head around. She felt like she couldn't afford to give her solution away and she was very attached to the $200,000 she'd invested up-front in developing the technology.

Rightly or wrongly, conversions are 80–90% percent higher for SaaS solutions (and many other online or mobile solutions) that offer a free trial period. If you look at similar products—cloud-based accounting software, file sharing, project management etc.—you will be hard pressed to find a company that doesn't offer a free trial on at least one of their packages. If your product or service is disruptive, high-tech, or unknown, you too will be likely to meet much more resistance at the old brain level and Step #6 will become pivotal. The old brain of your prospects is hardwired to keep you safe, and new or disruptive technologies pose a perceived threat. This, coupled with the fact that the new brain has been trained to be suspicious of offers that might cause you to lose money or get ripped off, makes it even more important to understand the concerns of your audience and the impediments to closing the sale.

Unless your technology solution is well known or the price point is very low, there is a high risk that you will lose a significant amount of your traffic at Step #6 without a risk free trial of some sort.

Chapter 13

In Alicia's case, it took two months of deliberation before she was prepared to take that step and re-engineer the sign-up offer and process. She bit the bullet and decided to offer a 30-day free trial on her base level package. The benefits of that decision started paying off within weeks. She recorded a 100% growth in sign-ups within two weeks and 480% within 60 days. With a few special offers, an induction video, and regular communications out to all these new members, she was able to achieve a conversion rate of just over 39% after the expiry of the free trial. This was an excellent result for Alicia—she was building a steady monthly income from paid memberships and she was also growing the database of prospects who were interested in her product but had not yet converted into paying customers.

Before moving on to the next and final chapter in our 7 Step Sales Seduction Process, take some time to discover which objectives or impediments are troubling your audience and blocking the sale. Next, make a list of possible solutions and commence testing those with a handful of prospects and existing customers. Remember, it is important to do the homework and not to guess or presume anything. Finally, actively solicit feedback and suggestions for each of the proposed solutions to determine which will be the most effective at helping more prospects to decide to step into your solution now.

> **KEY POINT**
> Good questions hold the answers to most of the shortcomings and rejection that you've experienced to date. By doing your homework, you make it harder for your prospect to think herself out of the sale.

What Do You Need Your Audience to Do Right Now?

Step #7—Compel Action

For once I was confused.

"What exactly do you want your customers to do?" I asked.

Talking to Matthew was like trying to hold on to a tornado. In his late twenties and fancying himself as the "ultimate ideas man", his mind was constantly on the move, sifting new concepts and exploring ways to tap into the potential of business networking. But, despite all his boundless energy and efforts, he felt he was missing something.

Pinning him down early one morning over breakfast, I asked him to clarify what he wanted to achieve with his website.

Matthew, his forkful of scrambled egg frozen in midair, looked puzzled.

"I thought I spelled it out pretty clearly on my homepage," he replied matter-of-factly. "Our website provides our clients with plenty of options—products for sale, valuable free information, and cutting-edge networking events specifically designed to help them survive this challenging economic climate. I don't know what more I can possibly offer?"

"So it sounds like you have lots on offer but you're not getting the results you want?" I asked.

Having breakfast with Matthew was not conducive to good digestion. His eyes were constantly on the move, checking his phone, watching the time, noting the traffic—ALL as he rattled out new ideas and opportunities for expansion. He was exhausting, and after an hour with him I began to appreciate the expression, *"go home, take an aspirin and have a nice lie down."*

"I don't get it," he said, shaking his head. "I should be getting hundreds of sign-ups a day."

Matthew was referring to the e-newsletter subscription on his site. With excellent search engine optimization (SEO) and pay-per-click marketing (PPC) in place, he knew he was getting more than his fair share of unique visitors each day, but his database just wasn't growing. He needed to find a way to grow his list so that he had a solid stream of new prospects to talk to about his business networking products and services.

"What specifically are you asking your website visitors to do?" I asked.

"Oh, I've given them heaps of choices," Matthew replied. "I hate going to websites and finding nothing of interest. I'm off somewhere else in a flash. I saw this site the other—"

"So, what do you offer your visitors on the homepage?" I interjected, knowing I had to be firm or we'd still be there at lunchtime swirling around the surface of his problem.

"A little sample of every product and service we have," Matthew replied, looking at me oddly. "If I show them all the great stuff we have, surely something will catch their interest, and we are bound to get some good results."

"What does a good result look like?" I prompted.

"Well, for instance they might buy my e-book for $19.99," he replied, concentrating fully for a change. "I've got podcasts for sale, they can subscribe to my blog to get free tips, and there's a series of eight webinars they can sign up for. Then down below that, I also make it really easy for them to check out our latest social media feeds and I have a whole section on our huge selection of networking events. We have the largest selection of networking events, with something to suit almost every niche—high-tech, men only, women only, home-based business, professional services, and retail. And I also have an app I'm developing as well."

It seemed like the perfect storm and Matthew was right in the middle of it.

"So, if I went to your site right now," I asked, "what is it that you'd hope I would focus on and do?"

"Well," Matthew said, "at the very least, I would like you to sign up for my newsletter."

"Matthew," I said, quietly, "do you know what a call to action is?"

"Of course," he grinned. "I have lots of them on my homepage."

"Yes, you do," I agreed. "But how am I supposed to know which one (out of the eight that you have given me) you want me to do?"

That's the funny thing about being in the eye of the storm. It's easy to get caught up and carried away by your own flurry of ideas, products, and services. You begin to think that you need to communicate every point and offer in your head to move your prospects toward a decision. But all you are really doing is creating a torrential flood that sweeps your audience further away from a decision to buy. And Matthew is not the only entrepreneur to fall victim to a cyclone of his own making. At some point in their career, virtually every business owner and senior marketer will fail to close an important deal simply because they have given their prospect too many choices. Sometimes giving your audience too many choices is far worse than giving a weak call to action or no call at all.

The competence to close the sale or finish your marketing message with a strong call to action is the final but second most important step in the Sales Seduction Process—the most important step of course being Step #1, capturing attention up-front and holding it throughout.

Everything that you have learned and done so far in Part 2 of this book has brought you to the point where you have now earned the right to ask for the sale. Since you have done the hard work and made it easier for your audience to say "Yes" to what you do, now is a good time to get out of your own way. Do yourself a favor and pay special attention to the simplicity and effortless flow of Step #7 in the Sales Seduction Process—Compel Action. Yes, you must ask for the sale but no, you do not have to force or compel it by memorizing sophisticated closing techniques. The sale is not about you and your linguistic prowess. It is about the buyer and his willingness to step into the solution that ends his pain once and for all.

> **KEY POINT**
> **Your mission is simply to make it easy for your**
> **prospect to decide and step into the solution.**

Chapter 14

Before we look at the different options that are available to compel action and discover what Matthew did to create a massive boost to his results, let's do a brief recap of where we are at so far in the 7 Step Sales Seduction Process:

- You have done your homework up-front to identify, measure, and rank your prospect's pain so that you can create a message that grabs and holds his attention

- You have presented a clear visual representation up-front of how your solution can impact his world

- Your prospect knows that he is not alone and that you can help him to solve this common problem once and for all

- You have stated clear, succinct, and tangible claims that let him know which specific pain you provide THE solution for

- You have proven that your solution will produce a net gain and solve his pain

- All impediments and concerns blocking the sale have been removed

And if you have managed to skillfully complete each of these six steps, now is the perfect time to close or ask for the sale. However, to do this effectively, you must first bring the old brain of your prospect back to full attention. If you recall our discussion in Part 1, Chapter 5, unless your message is very short (less than one minute) it is impossible to keep your audience at 100% attention throughout. In order to deliver a call to action that is remembered and triggers a decision, the old brain of your prospect must be alert and attentive.

So you must be wondering, *"How exactly do you go about waking him up or ensuring that his old brain is in the most receptive state?"*

For those of you who have chosen to open your sales or marketing message with a client story, a dramatization, or a metaphor to capture attention, now would be a good time to finish that story and use it as an opportunity to reinforce your key claims and gains. The reptilian brain of your prospect was paying full attention when you first introduced your characters and their familiar dilemma, so he'll be especially curious to perk up now and learn what happened in the end. Remember, the part of your prospect's brain that decides is looking for and paying special attention to the beginning and the end of everything.

If you have utilized an open ended question, word play, or controversial statement to intrigue your audience up-front, come back to it now and provide the answers or conclusions that the old brain is waiting to hear. If you are like Bill, the pharmaceutical sales representative in Chapter 8, and you used a prop (such as a pillow and a note) to grab attention, refer back to it now for added effect and emphasis. Make sure you use the opportunity to re-state your claim and the net gain the customer will achieve by choosing your solution now. Invite your audience to connect with that prop in some tangible way and wherever possible leave it physically with them. This same technique and formula will apply beautifully if you used a movie, a song, a texture, or a prototype in your bid to captivate attention up-front.

If you opened with a "before and after" photo (or asked your audience to build an image in their own mind), now is the perfect time to come back to it and highlight how it proves and fortifies your key points. Returning to something that is familiar and memorable from the beginning sends a strong message to the old brain of your audience that it is time to wake up and take note of what is being communicated. It's akin to putting a Post-it note, an asterisk, or an underline next to your final message in the brain of your potential customer.

> **KEY POINT**
> **Step #7—Compel Action is really about bringing the
> attention of your audience back to an alert and receptive
> state so that you can re-emphasize your key messages.**

Once you have done that, the close or call to action can really be achieved with a simple question or command, such as:

- Which suits you best for a start date, Tuesday or Thursday?

- How do you see my solution increasing X?

- Which is easier for you—Visa or MasterCard?

- How does that look to you?

- What's the most important insight you learned from what we discussed today?

- Call now to get started saving X.

- Grab your copy of X today.

- Click here to begin your trial.

Ideally, if you are in a sales situation, the close should be a question that invites them to step into the solution now. Direct your audience to focus on discussing the most important insight they will take away or how they see the solution impacting their world. Your mission is not to get them to say "Yes" or "No" but rather to inspire them to imagine their world now that they have purchased your solution. Closing becomes effortless when you put the focus on them and their need to solve the pain today. The magic is also more likely to happen if you have first laid a good foundation with Steps 1 through to 6—positioning your solution, proving it can solve your prospect's pain, and removing all impediments to a decision.

Chapter 14

Even if you are communicating a PR or marketing message in a print or digital environment, you must remember to ask for the sale. In most instances, you will likely find that a directive or command works best and gets straight to the point. Wherever possible, ask your audience to do one thing only. It is better to get a "No" to one specific call to action, than to ask your audience to do three different things and get no response at all.

And if you're not yet convinced, Matthew's networking venture and website is a classic example of how too many calls to action can overwhelm and confuse an audience into not deciding anything. He had over 400 pages of valuable content and roughly 8000 unique visitors a day, yet his database hadn't grown in the past 12 months and he sold very little product online. He was very successful at running networking events and showing business owners how to get the most out of each networking encounter, but his online business was a huge drain on both his time and money. He needed to turn it into a lead generation machine and he needed to do it quickly before it pulled the rest of his business under.

Thankfully, Matthew was sufficiently motivated to solve this problem. Once he decided that his number one priority was to build a strong database of customers to market his products, coaching programs, and events to, it became a whole lot easier for him to harness the hurricane on his homepage. He gained a whole new appreciation for the phrase "less is more". He found that by re-organizing his products, programs, free resources, and events, and shifting the bulk of his claims, proof, and calls to action for them onto separate pages, he was able to buy himself a large section of prime real estate on his homepage to drive e-newsletter subscriptions. Rather than diluting his focus on seven or eight competing messages, he homed in on the one that was most important to him on the homepage.

He was an excellent study and he understood the primary pain of his customer very well. Most of his clientele were small businesses with less than three employees and the owners were time poor and cash strapped. They desperately needed sales to keep their fledgling enterprises afloat and

Matthew offered a particularly unique solution—speed networking via an online forum.

What if you could get 5 new leads for your business right now without even leaving the comfort of your home or office?

If you've got 2 minutes to spare, I can show you right now how to make that happen and it won't even cost you a dime. Just enter your email details below and I will share with you a simple step-by-step process of how you can get more leads and sales starting today. Each day, 7 new businesses join our network, and a few of them would like to share their success stories with you right now.

In the end, Matthew's call to action was fairly understated. He laid the foundation well by doing his homework, capturing attention, offering the solution, proving it had worked for others, and making it easy for his browsers to accept his offer to help them. He didn't have to work hard to keep his audience alert, hard-sell them, or write four pages of copy to convince them to sign up.

By executing the 7 Step Sales Seduction Process brilliantly, he added 1284 new leads to his database in 45 days and he generated an additional $6498 per month from his speed networking forum. In just under two months he turned a website that was losing money into a new profit center that brought him a decent return on investment and a whole new list of prospects that were interested in learning more about how to network effectively.

And remember, to succeed in your message being recalled, understood, and acted upon, you must put almost all of your energy and attention on the first and last messages that your potential customers see, hear, and experience. If it is not said at the beginning or the end, it simply won't be remembered or done.

Chapter 14

To create campaigns that consistently close more business, you need to do your homework up-front and follow each step in the 7 Step Sales Seduction Process. The process was designed to ensure that you deliver the right information in the language of seduction to the decision making part of your audience's brain.

> **KEY POINT**
> **The 7 Step Process is the best way to ensure that you deliver the right message, at the right time, and in the right way to the old brain, so that you trigger a decision quickly.**

PART THREE

7 Impact Boosters That Amplify Your Influence

Now that you have mastered the 7 Stimuli That Charm the Old Brain and the 7 Steps That Help Your Prospects to Say "Yes", you're ready to learn some advanced techniques. This third set of tools—the 7 Impact Boosters That Amplify Your Influence—hold the power to magnify and multiply your results. The more of these impact boosters you can employ when designing and delivering your next message, the more immediate and intense the impact will be in the mind of your prospect. These principles will help you grab and retain attention, enhance retention, and trigger a quick decision.

Is Your Prospect Primed?

Impact Booster #1—The Priming Effect

Hugh, the owner of a regional chain of ten mattress and bedding stores, had his sheets in a real tangle. He'd been in business for more than seven years but he just wasn't seeing a return on his advertising dollar.

"Look at this," he exclaimed, handing me a thick, glossy catalogue. "I've spent thousands on the photography and printing and it's got me nowhere."

I admired the huge classic four-poster bed on the front cover and started to flick through the hundreds of beds and bedroom settings, which were presented together with an impressive amount of specifications and technical information.

CHAPTER

Hugh's stores were in high traffic locations and produced decent walk by traffic and sales, but he suspected his competitors were consistently outselling him and growing their market share. All of them had top quality print catalogues on offer—something he'd been reluctant to invest in until recently. Now he wished he'd never bothered.

"What a waste of money," he said, passing across a small selection of flyers that he had also recently printed. "I'm doing no better with my expensive letterbox drops either."

I glanced at the flyers and saw another sea of beds. Hugh had built a reputation for supplying high quality mattresses, bed frames, and linens at reasonable prices. He was proud of his efforts to make beds affordable, and the expertise and attention to detail of his in-store team were much appreciated by his loyal customers. Now his inherent good nature was wearing thin.

"What else can I do to attract more customers?" he asked.

"What's the first thing that comes to your mind when you look at this catalogue?" I responded, matching his question with an even better one.

Hugh leaned back in his chair and thought for a moment.

"Fulfilled," he shot back, smiling. "All my questions about beds have been answered—every single one."

"But do you feel sleepy and cozy? Do you feel like all you want to do is curl up between those lovely smooth, silky sheets, snuggle down, and sleep for a week?"

"Well," Hugh hesitated, flummoxed. "Not really. But I've included everything a buyer needs to know when they're looking for a bed. My guess is, all that touchy-feely stuff would come after the bed is delivered when they've had a chance to lie on it."

"Okay, Hugh, but why do think your customers want to buy new beds?" I enquired.

"That's easy," he replied. "Most of the time it's because they need a new one. Their old one is likely worn out or they just want a better night's sleep."

"So, what would be the most enticing image you could present to someone who's desperate for a restful sleep?"

Hugh looked at me blankly.

"Hugh, I see a lot of mattresses in your catalogue but what I don't see is any promise of a good night's sleep," I said flipping through the pages. "You've got a lot of information and naked mattresses here. Yet none of them make me realize how tired I am and how much I need a new bed so that I can finally get a decent rest."

Almost everyone will at some point in their life discover how hard it is to function without sufficient sleep. Chances are, as you are reading this right now you will be able to cast your mind back to a time when it happened to you and remember vividly what it felt like to be exhausted. You might remember yourself yawning while trying desperately to stay awake during a boring lecture at school. Or perhaps the incident was a bit more recent? Maybe you recall how embarrassed you were in that meeting, trying to cover your mouth out of courtesy while your incessant yawning triggered a cascade of sympathy yawns from your work colleagues. For those of you who are parents of infants right now, you know only too well what it's like to try to function on little or no sleep.

And before you finish reading this paragraph, it's highly likely you will yawn at least once. If you are reading this book in a public place, there is a very good chance that your yawn will set off an epidemic of gaping mouths and self-conscious smiles. That's because yawning is incredibly contagious. Just reading the word yawn (seven times in the past few sentences), seeing it, or hearing someone else yawn, makes you want to do it too. Some studies have even shown that yawning can trigger emotional and physical responses of being tired—that you will begin to question and analyze your own physical state if you catch yourself yawning.

But why is an involuntary act like yawning so infectious? You and I start yawning even before we are born and most creatures on the planet also do it. Some argue it is simply a reflex while others maintain there are physiological, evolutionary, or biochemical reasons why we respond automatically to the sight, sound, or mention of the word. Although there have been many theories and hypotheses about why we yawn and why it's so contagious (for humans, chimpanzees, and dogs), none have been empirically proven.

Several recent studies by independent teams (Garrett Norris of the University of Leeds, Atsushi Senju of the University of London, Molly Helt of the University of Connecticut, and Ivan Norscia of the University of Pisa) seem to support the claim that contagious yawning is based on your capacity to empathize, and the level of social bonding you have with the person or persons who yawned. Norris, Helt, and Senju tested the reactions of autistic and non-autistic children to videos of people yawning, and also to people who were simply moving their mouths. Both groups of kids yawned the exact same amount after viewing people moving their mouths.

However, the non-autistic children yawned much more frequently when watching clips of subjects actually yawning. The children with autism, a condition which impedes social interaction, communication, and empathy, yawned markedly less. In fact, as the severity of autistic symptoms increased, the children became less likely to respond with a contagious yawn. So there is now credible evidence to suggest that even an involuntary response like yawning can be influenced, biased, or compelled by emotions, words, images, symbols, or memories.

By now, you must be wondering what yawning has to do with selling more beds (or whatever product or service you currently offer). It has to do with a little known phenomenon called the priming effect.

Clinical research has demonstrated conclusively that priming can impact judgment, action, and decision making. You experience the priming effect when there is an increase in the speed or accuracy of a decision due to your prior exposure to biased information, images, sentiments, or statements. In fact, simply by planting the word yawn in your mind a moment ago, I demonstrated that I could get you to not only yawn but also influence those seated near you to respond as well.

> **KEY POINT**
> **Priming occurs where your decisions and actions are predisposed and influenced by context, visuals, words, emotions, and symbols.**

As you are now discovering, most of the drivers behind the choices and decisions you make every day are largely happening below the level of thought and consciousness. In addition to the 7 Stimuli That Charm the Old Brain, you are also often strongly influenced by context, symbols, and intangible factors that up until now have slipped under the radar and gone undetected by you.

Advertisers of fast food and snack items have relied heavily on the priming effect for decades to trigger automatic snacking of available food during TV viewing. Obesity is now arguably the fastest growing cause of disease and death in the Western World. Many health advocates believe that a significant contributing factor to this epidemic is the pervasiveness of TV advertising for sugar infused, calorie rich, low-nutrient foods. In 2009, Jennifer Harris, John Bargh, and Kelly Brownell of Yale University conducted a series of experiments with adults and children that proved TV advertising wields significant power to prime snacking behavior during and after exposure to food advertising. While both children and adults consumed more snack foods (not just the brands advertised) when exposed to food advertising, a whopping 45% of children consumed more after being exposed to advertising of food versus watching commercials for other products. Is it any wonder that the percentage of children and adolescents who are overweight has more than tripled in the past 30 years?

Evidence of the priming effect is all around you. It is the reason why presidents and prime ministers pose for photos while sitting behind a desk, surrounded by a flag, a photo of their family, and bookshelves full of leather-bound books. Without saying a word, they have already predisposed or influenced your opinion of their values, work ethic, and intelligence.

It explains why voters cast more politically conservative ballots if asked to attend polls in or near a church location, as opposed to those who vote near government or secular buildings. It also clarifies why participants exposed to a simple illuminated incandescent light bulb—an iconic image of insight—were four times more effective at solving problems requiring a creative solution than those in the control group who were not exposed to the light bulb.

> **KEY POINT**
> Your audience is persuaded not just by your physical sales or marketing message. To prime them to influence a decision in your favor, you can present subtle clues, biases, or context to steer their decisions and behavior.

If you remember, Hugh's catalogue (and his other direct mail and radio campaigns) featured a huge selection of beds and an equally large list of specifications and information. It's not a surprise that shoppers weren't exactly rushing in to buy their new mattress. Once Hugh discovered that he was in the business of solving pain, not selling the most comprehensive selection of beds, it completely changed his perspective on both the content and context of his advertising materials.

After doing the homework and working through Steps 1–7 of the Sales Seduction Process, Hugh was now ready to reshoot the images for his catalogue and flyers, and re-brief his graphic designer. He now knew that the number one source of pain for his customers was lack of (or interrupted) sleep, and that his customers were paying the price for it personally and financially. In most cases, they were highly motivated to find THE solution by the time they visited one of his stores. Hugh just had to get them to visit one of his locations.

The draft layout and artwork for his new catalogue were groundbreaking. Instead of trying to cram in every mattress and every piece of technical information, Hugh focused on the experience of getting a good night's sleep. He did a terrific job of grabbing attention up-front and presenting a clear "before and after" shot of a young family. But as I leafed through the draft copy, I couldn't help but feel that he had missed a valuable opportunity to boost the impact of his message by priming his audience. After all, lack of sleep is such a common and visceral source of pain. It would have been a shame for Hugh to stop just short of taking his message from wonderful to WOW!

We spent the next two weeks working with the graphic designer to bring the aura of a good night's sleep to Hugh's catalogue. Each key spread was carefully tweaked to ensure that Hugh visually conveyed the sensations of drowsiness, coziness, and restfulness. In the end, even the layout and the product descriptions were reminiscent of a bedtime story, but for adults! The copy was lightly peppered with the suggestions of yawning, and the designer took the "Z" from Hugh's last name and turned it into a new logo that she could use on each page of his print materials. And since most people automatically associate a good night's sleep with the symbol "Zzz", his audience was perfectly primed to be more predisposed to his key claim and message.

Hugh supplemented his new print advertising with an effective 30-second radio spot during the busy morning drive timeslot (6am to 9am). He got to speak directly to thousands of peak-hour commuters at the time when they felt their sleep deprivation the most and were, therefore, most likely to be receptive to the solution. His soothing message was delivered slowly in whisper tones with two long, drawn-out yawns and several mentions of the word yawn. Just listening to the simple, relaxing message made you wonder why you were up so early and what you'd be willing to trade for just 30 more minutes in bed under the covers. It primed the audience perfectly to respond to his simple call to action.

Hugh saved 50% by redesigning and refocusing his print advertising through his new catalogue and flyers. By resisting the urge to include too much, he focused only on what was most important to his customers, and he proved he could solve their number one pain. He used the advanced technique of priming to predispose his prospects to his message. By further drawing attention to their lack of sleep, his prospects became more likely to visit one of his stores in search of the solution. Once there, the expertise and resourcefulness of the sales team kicked in to help them find a perfect night's sleep. That's why in a six-month period Hugh was rewarded handsomely with a lift in sales of 112%.

Take some time today to think about how you can apply this advanced message boosting principle to your ads, your website, your catalogue, your next email, or even your packaging. Bear in mind the feeling, mood, or mindset you want your audience to be in when they hear your message. You have many tools at your disposal—music, images, words, emotions, symbols, memories, metaphors, and context—to increase the speed or accuracy of your prospect's decision. And remember, these cues are most successful when they are subtle and below the level of thought and consciousness. If your message is too overt or obvious, you may actually provoke, instead of priming, your prospects.

Priming is a very powerful motivating force. Just as Bill made use of a pillow in a box (in Chapter 8) or Hugh employed his "Zzz" symbol to bias and influence his sleep deprived shoppers, you have an amazing opportunity to

Chapter 15

give your audience a gentle nudge in the right direction and set them up to be more receptive to respond and say "Yes" to your sales or marketing message.

> **KEY POINT**
> Priming works when your cues are subtle and below the level of thought and consciousness. Your intent should be to prime, not provoke, your prospects—avoid using cues or suggestions that are overt or obvious.

Chapter 15

Is Your Message Moving Them?

Impact Booster #2—Movement

Travis is a walking advertisement for his business. In his mid-thirties, with a stylish but not overly trendy haircut, confident walk, and abs to die for, he radiates health. Not surprisingly, Travis owns and operates a large suburban gym, attracting local mums during the day and a quick in-and-out business crowd in the early mornings and evenings.

Taking a seat in the gym's comfortable coffee lounge, Travis handed me one of his signature green fitness drinks.

"What do you think?" he asked, gesturing boldly around the room with his arms wide open.

CHAPTER

He'd just taken me on a tour of the facilities and I was suitably impressed. In fact, the energy and momentum were so infectious, I wanted to race home and grab my trainers and sprint back to join in on all the fun.

"It's one of the most female-friendly gyms I've been in," I enthused. "I don't feel like I'm in an old-school meat market or somewhere I need to purchase a $300 outfit just to work out in. It just feels comfortable and accessible for patrons at every fitness level. You've managed to strike a really great balance here for both men and women."

Travis had managed to utilize the space very well to cater to his diverse clientele. His most spacious studio space was decked out to accommodate Pilates, yoga, step classes, and spin sessions, depending on the demand and the time of day. He had a great spread of cardio equipment with a bird's eye view of the beach, a separate weight room, sauna, spa, and a heated lap pool. He even provided on-site childcare facilities for parents with children under seven years of age.

"Am I missing something that gym-goers need?" Travis asked, looking concerned.

"Why do you ask?" I questioned. "You've got a fantastic facility with something for everyone."

Taking some flyers off the coffee table in front of us, Travis handed me two of them for review.

"I've letterbox dropped these into the local residential area," Travis said, with a defeated sigh. "Being close to the water and the city, this suburb is fairly affluent and I know most of my female clientele live within a 10km radius. For them, I use the flyer that mentions the childcare facility—to entice them to come in during the day when we are quiet. The second one is more targeted toward single professionals who live around here but commute and work in the city. In that one, I focus on the convenience of dropping in, the early and late hours of operation, the ease of getting on the cardio equipment, and the chance to meet other singles. I'm beginning to wonder if I have the wording and photos wrong, because for some reason these flyers just aren't working."

Travis had a sure-fire way to know if his campaign was successful or not. By offering a 20% discount if a new member brought in one of these flyers or quoted the special coupon code, he could track the strike rate and measure the return on his investment. So far, his return on investment over the past five months was pretty poor—less than 4%. He knew the message was getting out there but he also knew it wasn't getting noticed or taken up.

I held up the flyer he was sending out to attract women with young children and opened it so that Travis could see it clearly.

"Let's take a look at your flyer and then compare it to what you see when you look around your facilities," I said.

Smiling, Travis did as I asked.

"Okay," he said, grinning. "Now what?"

"What's the key difference between what's happening here at the gym and what you have portrayed in the flyer?" I asked, continuing to hold the flyer in front of him.

Travis frowned.

"I don't follow you," he said. "I have done the best I could with words and photos to show mothers what they're missing out on—having some 'me' time while the kids are looked after, getting back into shape, and meeting new friends."

"Yes, you have," I agreed. "But what haven't you shown them? What can't they see and hear about your fitness centre that is even more compelling?"

Travis stared at the flyer and then shrugged.

"I have no idea. I'm not sure I understand what you're getting at."

"Well, the first thing I noticed about your club was the energy and movement," I smiled. "When I look around I see members powering forward on treadmills, limbs stretching in yoga poses, friends encouraging each other and visiting, weights being lifted, personal trainers helping clients achieve their goals—the action and activity is infectious. The music, the momentum, it makes me want to start a workout—right now."

Travis kept his eyes on the flyer.

"But it's really hard to put action onto a piece of paper," he protested, shaking his head.

"Well, that may or may not be true," I replied. "But it's virtually impossible to motivate a woman to get off her duff and exercise with a message that is lifeless and devoid of movement."

If there is one thing that I know for sure, it's that a body in motion tends to stay in motion. A body on the couch watching TV and eating cheese puffs, however, tends to stay on the couch. It's a simple law of physics.

Similarly, your old brain is hardwired to pay attention to and prefer motion. In the case of your ancestors, this bias kept them alive. It allowed them to detect or distinguish potential prey, and it simultaneously kept them safely out of the jaws of predators. And not much has changed in thousands of years.

Even right now as you read and concentrate on this book, your old brain is still scanning the room for potential dangers. That's why even the slightest movement—the lights from a car passing by your house, a person walking by your office window, or even a pet wandering into the room—will catch your eye and cause your thoughts and attention to be diverted. Movement is a powerful and persuasive tool that, when used in conjunction with the 7

Steps That Help Your Prospects to Say "Yes", can help boost your influence and effectiveness significantly.

According to research done in both the United Kingdom and the United States, movement of the eyes from side to side improves memory. While there is still some speculation as to why memory is enhanced, Andrew Parker and his colleagues at the Manchester Metropolitan University found that subjects who were presented with a list of words while following a computer prompt that initiated side-to-side eye movements had 10% greater recall than subjects who only heard the words, or those who were prompted to move their eyes up and down.

Since the right side of the brain is normally associated with long-term memory and the left side with short-term memory, it is entirely plausible that the side-to-side motion causes the two hemispheres to communicate and interact with each other. It is also conceivable that the movement is triggering the old brain and assisting you to record, catalogue, and retrieve memories in specific brain cells. Irrespective of why it works, we now have proof that horizontal eye movement—which can be encouraged by the use of rotating banners, dynamic content, and video—enhances your ability to remember what you are exposed to.

KEY POINT
In order to create a message that compels action, it must first be noticed and remembered. If you can incorporate motion into your message or its delivery, you can significantly boost impact, recall, and action.

Words also have the power to move you and your audience in more ways than one. While most of you now associate the words (or copy) of your message with the domain of the neocortex (the thinking part of your brain), scientists have recently discovered that powerful narratives can influence and activate other parts of your brain and physiology as well. For example,

Chapter 16

fMRI research has found that participants who read words with strong odor associations generated robust responses in multiple brain centers—their neocortex and primary olfactory cortex (where smells are processed) both lit up. Similarly, a team from Emory University in 2012 revealed that when subjects were exposed to a story depicting texture and tactile references, the sensory cortex (responsible for deciphering information related to touch and feel) was activated.

When it comes to movement, it has been proven that words describing motion stimulate both the language processing areas and the motor cortex which regulates the body's movement and actions. Véronique Boulenger of the Laboratory of Language Dynamics scanned the brains of her subjects as they read sentences like, "Marc grasped the racquet," and "Ava kicked the ball." Those scans clearly revealed activity not only in the neocortex, but also in the motor cortex. In fact, a very specific part of the motor cortex that relates to arm movement lit up for the first sentence, while a different section that correlates to leg movement became active when the participants read that Ava kicked a ball.

Just as Dr. Maxwell Maltz, one of the forefathers of modern day neuroscience, proposed back in 1960, the brain doesn't distinguish between what is read, imagined, or experienced in real life. When presented with a sales or marketing message that clearly describes or illustrates movement, the same neurological regions of your brain are stimulated as if you were experiencing or performing that behavior or action yourself. Similarly, when you present a message that inspires activity, your prospect's brain will automatically engage the parts of his brain that control movement. So movement is vital to making your message more compelling and successful.

KEY POINT
Words have the power to move you and your audience. If you want to enhance the persuasiveness of your message, choose words and descriptors that simulate or incite movement.

Movement also imitates real life and as you learned in Chapters 6 and 7 (creating a clear picture and an emotional connection), the old brain is enchanted with messages and mediums that emulate reality. It's one of the reasons why TV viewing and advertising have been so strong over the past few decades. It's also the reason why we have seen exponential growth in the viewing and influence of video on the internet.

According to a Nielsen Report released in 2012, almost 145 million people in the US watch videos online and a whopping 290 million watch TV. Most Americans reportedly spend 32 hours and 47 minutes a week watching TV.

The penetration of online video is already at 50% of the TV watching public and growing steadily at a far greater rate than TV viewing. These statistics are also consistent with what is happening in other developed nations like Canada, Australia, the United Kingdom, and Japan. While the time spent on the internet seems low at only 3 hours and 58 minutes a week, the figures have more than doubled in the past three years. Other independent agencies estimate the Nielsen numbers to be overly conservative—with reports of up to 182 million US internet users online and an average of 5 hours and 40 minutes a week spent viewing videos.

If you assume the average person is awake for 17 hours a day, that leaves you with roughly 120 hours a week to eat, work, travel, engage in recreation, and take care of domestic or family responsibilities. Yet the statistics clearly show that most of you are spending 26–30% of that time either watching TV or viewing videos. That's a significant amount of your waking hours spent in front of a screen and a clear indication of how powerful and pervasive this medium is. It is all-encompassing because the movement in TV and video captivates your attention and simulates real life. It draws you in and paints a clear picture of what life would be like, say, if you lived on the third floor of a small apartment in Pasadena, across the hallway from two physics nerds named Sheldon and Leonard. It shows you exactly how your health would be different, or what would be possible, if you started taking the same vitamin supplement as Jillian Michaels.

> **KEY POINT**
> **Movement is incredibly convincing because it imitates real life. If TV advertising is out of your reach, consider incorporating video into your sales or marketing message to boost your impact.**

So let's come back now to Travis and his all too familiar marketing dilemma. Travis was in a very enviable position of having a high energy, active product but he was stuck in the rut of trying to communicate it in a motionless, flat medium. As a relatively small business, he had several options: (1) find a way to bring life and movement to his marketing flyer, (2) introduce video as a communication vehicle, or (3) some combination of the first two alternatives.

After working his way through Steps 1–7 of the Sales Seduction Process, Travis gained some constructive clarity about the pain his customers were in and what he needed to do to solve it. He also got very clear about his claims, and what he needed to do to prove the net gain to his prospects so he could generate more leads and close more memberships. However, the greatest lessons came from his discovery of the power of customer testimonials (as a method of proof) and the intoxicating lure of movement in the old brain of his prospects.

Equipped with this valuable information, Travis was in an excellent position to re-engineer the flyer he sent out to young mothers, and introduce a whole series of videos to showcase what life would be like once they purchased his solution. Instead of filling his brochure with photos of the gym's equipment and a laundry list of classes, packages, and options, Travis focused on what mattered most to women with young children—they just wanted to get back to their pre-pregnancy weight and feel good about themselves.

Therefore, he opted to tell a story that they could relate to, and in doing so he captured their attention up-front, established commonality, and moved them forward (both physically and emotionally) in their journey from mother and caregiver to self-confident and fit woman. Instead of filling his flyer with information and photos, he focused solely on the character in his story, and he directed his audience to a video link (a short URL that was easy to type) with five customer testimonials that showcased the results each woman had achieved in the past six months. Here is an excerpt from Travis's updated brochure:

Hey You on the Couch Eating Potato Chips!

Yes, you! I'm talking to you because I know exactly what it's like to be a mother of young children and to feel like there's not enough time in the day to take care of YOUR body AND manage work, household chores, and the needs of your children. In fact, since we're on the subject, when's the last time you got out for a 30-minute walk in the sunshine, swam a few laps in a pool, or just took an hour out to stretch your tired, aching back muscles ...

To hear from five of our customers, women who live right here in your neighborhood, visit this link to see where they have come from and what they have achieved in just 6 short months!

www.ABCfitness.com/...

Prior to the revamp, Travis was lucky to get 40 new leads a month from his promotional efforts. Three months in, he was happy to report that he had received 627 new enquiries, and that 203 optimistic mothers had joined as members. And for those of you who are wondering, Travis did some split testing of his flyer with and without the URL link to the video. In addition to receiving great feedback about how powerful and moving the testimonials were, he also measured a 39% higher response rate from women who received the link to the video.

Along the way, Travis also discovered that it is surprisingly easy and inexpensive to shoot, edit, and upload videos to the internet. The videos became a compelling and tangible way for him to introduce potential customers to his personal trainers, exercise tips, and possible options to meet their fitness goals in a relaxed and supportive environment.

Even if you're not in the business of selling fitness or an action-based product or service, movement can boost your cut-through, retention, and results. As you have just discovered, your choice of words and descriptors can go a long way toward moving your prospect from where they are to saying "Yes" to your offer. Where you can, ask questions or use language that requires your audience to picture or imagine themselves recreating the problem and then stepping into the solution. Stories and metaphors are a particularly powerful way to draw the reader in and engage other regions of your prospect's mind that control body movement and action. Remember, these techniques are effective because the mind cannot distinguish between what is read, imagined, or experienced.

If your message is being delivered via the internet, PowerPoint, or some other digital medium, consider introducing dynamic graphics, rotating banners, interactive screens, or video to grab attention and increase recall. Where appropriate, use video to supplement and enhance the impact of your claims, gain, or proof. Video is by far the most powerful and cost effective way to captivate and convince the old brain because it is the closest thing to a real life experience.

Take some time before moving on to the next chapter to review your sales and marketing collateral and identify your best opportunities to instigate action and movement.

KEY POINT
Movement is a powerful and persuasive tool that when used in conjunction with the 7 Steps That Help Your Prospects to Say "Yes" can boost your influence and effectiveness tenfold.

Chapter 16

Are Eyes Really the Window to Your Soul?

Impact Booster #3—Put Your Best Face Forward

I found myself standing outside Katrina's shop in what should have been *the* prime location for a fashion retailer. She was conveniently positioned on the ground floor of a well established suburban shopping center, next to a high traffic anchor tenant and only 300 meters from the food court. When she called me in a panic about her lagging sales, I invited her to meet me out front at 1pm on Saturday—a time at which I suspected her target

C H A P T E R

demographic, the 14 to 17-year-old fashionistas, would be out in droves with money to burn.

"See," Katrina said. "There are hundreds of girls walking past the shop, but very few are taking note of our front window display or walking in to browse the racks and make a purchase. What am I missing?"

Katrina was a visual arts graduate and it showed in her elaborate front window display. It was artistic, full of color, and the clothes were right on trend with her target market. She had worked extremely hard over the last five months to catch their attention and lure them in, but today she was facing the very real prospect of defaulting on her rent and losing her coveted, high-traffic position.

"That's an interesting display," I murmured. "I love the skirt and singlet combos you've put together, and those Ed Hardy inspired, tattooed T-shirts really work well with your ghetto themed backdrop."

Katrina smiled.

"Thanks," she said. "I source my stock very carefully and do a lot of market research on trends and buying habits. Having two teen daughters also helps a lot."

"Their idea?" I asked, pointing at the simulated brick wall at the back of the display, which was riddled with graffiti, shiny CD discs, and popular album covers.

"Yes," Katrina laughed. "The girls love their music and they thought the colors and references to the latest bands and music would be super cool. I'd have never thought of that myself."

As edgy and visually striking as it was, there was something bothering me about her storefront display. It was creative and almost everyone who walked past turned their head to take note of the colors or the reflection of light off the CDs. But, like them, I wasn't connecting with the products for some reason and the display didn't draw me into her store.

"Katrina," I said turning my back on the shop, "your mannequins are really unusual, aren't they?"

"Yes, yes, they are," she replied enthusiastically. "I spent a lot of time thinking that through. I wanted them to be really edgy and eclectic."

They were interesting for sure. Katrina had removed the heads completely and replaced them with her own artistic creations made out of old vinyl records and various metal pieces. But without faces that looked familiar, her mannequins looked foreign and inhuman.

"Is this a new look you are trying out, or have you been using this approach for a while?" I asked, bringing up the homepage of her website on my tablet. "Let's have a look at your online merchandising."

"Our online site has never been a big money-maker," Katrina said, as we navigated to the pages that showcased her collection. "Plenty of visitors, and they seem to stay for a few minutes having a look, but hardly any sales."

Her creativity had definitely extended to her online presence. I saw a good balance between text and images, large detailed product photos, and some great suggestions to help browsers mix and match tops, bottoms, and accessories. Guessing that Katrina's art degree would have made her handy with a camera, I complimented her on the product photography.

"Hmm," she murmured, nodding. "It was the best I could do without professional models. They're way too expensive. I just thought through the best color combinations and shot the products lying flat on a white background. It took a while but I was still able to capture the color, texture, and features of each garment pretty well."

"That's an interesting choice, seeing as how you've got two teenage daughters and their friends," I reminded her.

Katrina looked at me quizzically.

"But who is going to want to see the garments on the girls?" she quipped. "They wouldn't know how to stand properly. Plus I've seen this technique used by hundreds of retailers online and in catalogues and it seemed like the next best choice to hiring real models. Do you think it really makes that much of a difference?"

"At the end of the day, it doesn't really matter what you and I think," I surmised. "If your teenage shoppers aren't pulling out their wallets and snapping up your separates like clearance items at a Boxing Day sale, then it must matter to the *real* decision maker—their old (or reptilian) brain."

Even if you are not in the business of selling clothing, I'm willing to bet that at some point in your life you have bought an outfit or two. If you've ever gone shopping either online or in-store, no doubt you will have come into contact with a mannequin or a photo of a model wearing the items that you were interested in. And chances are you were more influenced by that experience than you realize. Most of you will not have consciously taken note of anything in particular, but the part of your brain that decides is highly reliant (for your survival) on your ability to recognize and read faces. It pays attention to every face it sees and even those, as in the case of Katrina's headless mannequins, that are notably absent.

So it begs the question, "How important is it that you put your best face forward in your sales and marketing message?"

Your ability to recognize faces is probably something you've never stopped to think about or question. But as you navigate your day, you rely incessantly on your brain's ability to identify and remember faces. Just think of all the times you asked your brain to help you with this task today—you waved hello to a neighbor on your way to work, you looked for your work colleagues at the coffee shop, you caught your own reflection in the mirror, or you may have even greeted an old friend on the street. If you could not easily differentiate between all of these unique faces, wouldn't your life be complicated and confusing?

Unfortunately, those who suffer from face blindness live in a constant state of bewilderment. Face blindness is a rare medical condition that affects a person's temporal lobe—the part of the brain that recognizes faces. People with this challenging condition can see each individual part of a person's face—the nose, the eyes, the cheekbones, the mouth—but they are unable to put them all together and make one clear, recognizable picture. In severe cases, sufferers cannot even recognize themselves or the people they have known all their lives. In order to make sense of their world and stay safe, they are forced to rely on other cues like voices, clothing, words (name tags), touch, and smell.

If your temporal lobe is operating right now as it should, your brain will recognize faces by identifying and analyzing each individual part and then constructing an overall map or barcode. According to a 2009 study in the *Journal of Vision*, your brain sees every face as a series of shapes, lines, and areas of lightness or shadow. Your brain scans all the information you see in milliseconds just like a barcode, and it allows you to know in an instant if the person is a friend or a stranger. In fact, this function is considered so important to your survival that the type of and speed of processing that occurs in your brain to recognize faces is different and faster than it is for all other objects you encounter.

Your brain is hardwired to prioritize the measurement of another person's intent. To do this, your brain gives preference to visual stimuli that allow you to clearly make out facial features and determine whether a person is safe or intends to do you harm. Essentially, your brain does a quick database search through a collection of facial expressions you have amassed over a lifetime and decides which meaning or purpose to ascribe to the face you have just encountered—worried, angry, suspicious, excited, threatening, frustrated, or exasperated etc. When your brain cannot determine the intention quickly and easily, it has to work harder, and this uses up valuable energy and delays the decision making process.

KEY POINT
If you want to decrease your sales cycle and make it easier for your prospect to decide, present a face that is familiar and easy to interpret.

For those of you who use models, mannequins, celebrity endorsements, photographs of customers, videos etc. this knowledge is invaluable. In addition to the 7 Stimuli That Charm the Old Brain, you must also pay special attention to the face you put forward in your message. If you or your team members speak directly to your customers, your number one objective is to create a safe and comfortable environment. If you are nervous, frustrated, or stressed about the sale, chances are your prospect will pick this up, albeit unconsciously, and be less open to hearing what you have to say. If your marketing, merchandising, or packaging contains images of others, ensure that the expressions on these faces are congruent with the emotion and message you want to get across. If the face you are using in your collateral is currently ambiguous, obstructed, or missing, you may want to reconsider your strategy in light of what you now know about the old brain's predisposition for interpreting facial cues.

And just before you get too comfortable thinking that this knowledge only applies to human faces, there's some interesting research that suggests it can also be extrapolated to designs that contain facial elements (i.e. eyes, nose, mouth), illustrations of faces, and animal characters. Recently, a company in the US has conducted a study which suggests this tendency of your brain to home in on facial cues is also directly correlated to higher customer engagement and sales of products that have stylized facial design elements.

Mimoco is a company that designs and sells designer USB flash drives. While the generic version may retail from $8–$35, the Mimoco motifs, which range from "Hello Kitty" to "Star Wars", command $20–$70 in specialty boutiques, high-end department stores, and online retailers. The pressure was on management to find new and exciting designs that would captivate the attention of their tech-savvy, fashion conscious customers. Therefore, Mimoco engaged an outside agency to measure emotional engagement of their existing designs by equipping subjects with a biometric monitoring system—a chest band (similar to the device worn by runners for monitoring their pulse) with multiple biometric sensors to detect motion, heart rate, respiration, and skin conductivity. Eye-tracking was also used to supplement the basic biometric measures.

What they discovered was that there was a strong connection between the designs that evoked high emotional responses in the participants and those that achieved higher sales. Out of a selection of 30 designs that were already in-market with established sales performance, the testing correctly revealed four out of the five top performing characters. According to the researchers, there were several key elements of note that were consistent amongst the designs that generated the highest sales. The top performers all featured large eyes, a bold color palette, and tended to "express an attitude or strong intention". Conversely, the inverse of these attributes (small or no eyes, muted colors, and vacant stares) tended to generate both low emotional engagement and poor sales.

This biometric research was also subsequently backed up by testing of online ads for a selection of 30 new proposed USB designs. Notably, the designs with high emotional engagement (based on biometric testing) generated twice as many clicks as the less engaging counterparts.

> **KEY POINT**
> Even if the face you present to your audience is stylized
> or unconventional, ensure that the eyes are prominent
> and that the overall feeling or intent draws your prospects
> in emotionally and makes them feel connected to and
> engaged with you and your product or service.

So what does this all have to do with your sales and marketing message? In order to influence and persuade your audience, you must do four things well:

- Capture attention

- Let them know it is safe for them to deal with you so you can deliver your message

- Boost recall

- Trigger the old brain to decide

If your audience cannot connect with the face of your message (whether that is you, your team members, your images, your packaging, or your merchandising), it is unlikely that you will capture her attention and establish that it is safe to be with you. If you have failed on either of the first two steps, it will be even more difficult to get your prospect to commit your message to memory because she won't have the requisite level of emotional engagement. And it will be very difficult to get her to say "Yes" to your product or service if she's not engaged and she can't remember your message.

Perhaps this is the scientific proof we have been looking for to corroborate the old adage "the eyes are the window to the soul"? We as humans are fascinated by faces and our brains are hardwired to prioritize the measurement of another's intent. Knowing this, there can be no better argument or substantiation for the importance of Impact Booster #3— Put Your Best Face Forward. That's why it's imperative when designing your next sales presentation, advertisement, email, website, packaging, or display, to draw your audience in and create an emotional connection with compelling facial cues.

And in the case of Katrina, with her headless mannequins and still shots of clothing laid out flat for her website, the oversight of Impact Booster #3 was detrimental to both customer engagement and sales. Thankfully, it was a mistake that was very easy to rectify. She went to work that very afternoon to re-merchandise and bring a familiar face, and some humanity, back to her storefront window and in-store displays. It took a little longer, about three weeks in total, to reshoot all of her clothing on models and upload the new images to her website.

When I caught up with her again outside her shop, the impact of the changes was plain for everyone to see. Her business was on the mend and her cash flow pressures (and stress) had eased substantially. There was a real buzz about the store and her sales team had renewed energy and passion. She measured an impressive 41% increase in traffic and a 28% increase in sales. She also got a lot of positive feedback on her new window from both customers and her neighboring retailers. No one could put their finger on what was different exactly, but they definitely knew they liked what they saw.

Online sales were taking a bit longer than she had expected to pick up, but she was pleased to report that the amount of time each shopper stayed on her site was up by 1.73 minutes, and the average number of items per basket had increased from 1 to 2.61. With a few more adjustments and some investment in driving more traffic online, Katrina could definitely imagine the website being a great asset for sales and brand awareness.

Chapter 17

KEY POINT
Your audience is fascinated by faces and their brains are hardwired to prioritize the measurement of human intent. When designing your next sales presentation, advertisement, email, testimonial, packaging, or display, use strong facial images and indicators to draw your audience in, create an emotional connection, and boost recall.

Where Have I Heard That Before?

Impact Booster #4—Repetition

When it comes to questions or concerns I have about nutrition and grooming for my cat Samurai, I have my go-to guy, Ben. Recommended by my local veterinarian when he suggested some dietary changes, Ben is the owner of my neighborhood pet store and a goldmine of information. Tall, lanky, and passionate about pet care, with a head of hair that would put a purebred sheep dog to shame, he even looks like an animal lover.

CHAPTER
18

He was busy with customers when I arrived, so I had a chance to do one of my favorite things—wander to the back of the shop to admire and cuddle the kittens and puppies. As always, the runs were immaculate, with plenty of water on hand, and the little fluff balls smelled of shampoo as I held one close to my chest and buried my cheek in the fur at the nape of his neck.

Ten minutes later, Ben joined me.

"They always look so happy and lively," I commented, putting the fluffy white kitten with incredible blue eyes back in with his playful littermates.

Ben smiled. "Yes," he said. "As you know, they're well looked after and loved from the day they arrive. All I've got to do is convince their new owners that nutritional care is just as important as lots of love and exercise."

"Is that a problem?" I asked.

Ben shrugged and gestured toward the colorful posters and information sheets covering the walls.

"There's so much information and so many choices," he said. "It's not like it was in the old days when most people bought their pet food in cans or bags at the grocery store. A lot of research has been dedicated to improving nutrition and increasing the longevity of our pets. We now know that some additives that have been used for years to increase the shelf life of pet food are quite harmful to our four-legged friends. Most owners have no idea that the food they are feeding their pets right now is full of preservatives, fillers, steroids, antibiotics, and hormones. They think that because the brand they have chosen is expensive or popular, that it is safe. I would estimate that 95% of owners out there have no idea what they are really feeding their pets, or whether it is safe or appropriate for their age, breed, or dietary requirements."

"Do most pets have special needs?" I asked.

Ben thought for moment.

"Well," he replied, "dogs and cats are just as susceptible to allergies, disease, and accidents as humans. They're prone to eating things they have found on the floor and they are often allowed far more indulgences." Ben laughed. "Not mentioning any names, but I know a pet owner who wouldn't allow her grandchildren to sit on the good furniture, yet her two Chihuahuas have free rein to scamper all over it with their dirty little paws. And when it comes to the right food and exercise, she doesn't have a clue. Both dogs are overweight, suffer from diabetes, and rarely get outside the yard for a good walk or a run in the park. She just doesn't understand that the right food can help prevent illness and disease, *and* add years to the lives of her beloved dogs."

"There certainly are some chunky pooches out there," I agreed.

"Yes," Ben enthused. "The right diet and exercise work wonders. Pets are a bit like humans in that way. If you overfeed your goldfish, it'll die quite quickly. But if you give your dog food from the table and snacks all the time, it'll develop a serious medical condition and will cost you a whole lot of money in veterinary consultations and medications. I really wish pet owners could see that they are harming their pets by not providing proper nutrition."

"Do you have a blog?" I asked. "That would be an effective way for you to get the word out and educate pet owners about the best alternatives for different breeds and specific conditions."

Ben nodded.

"Sure do," he said. "It's a really lively discussion place too."

"On pet health?" I queried. "I'm not surprised."

"Well, sort of," Ben responded. "More animal health and well-being really. I'm pretty fired up about live animal imports into various countries, and other things like baby seal slaughter, whale hunting, and illegal poaching of elephant tusks. Don't even get me started on the topic of dog fighting. There are a lot of criminal practices that should be looked into—you can tell my posts hit a nerve by all the passionate comments I get from animal rights activists."

"So, if you are busy with all those causes online, how do you spread the word about domestic pet care and nutrition to potential customers?" I asked.

Ben guided me over to his desk where he pulled up his website and began to scroll through the pages and pages of blog entries. There were literally hundreds.

"Oh, I cover that too. As you can see, I cover it all in my blog. I've got categories and keyword tags for almost every topic related to pets," he said proudly.

"But isn't your speciality domestic pet care and nutrition?" I asked.

"Yes, of course," he retorted. "But wouldn't my customers find it boring if that's all that I covered in the blog?"

"Perhaps," I suggested. "But at least they would know and remember what you do. There would be no confusion about that."

As a business owner, the biggest disservice that you can do is to try to "cover it all". By covering it all, you end up covering nothing very well. It's a bit like trying to paint the inside of an entire house with only one can of paint. You might be able to do it but none of the walls would look very good.

In today's challenging business environment, your target audience is bombarded with thousands of marketing messages every day. In order to create cut-through and present a clear and coherent brand message, that message has to be the same every single time someone experiences it. To be effective, you cannot afford to be all things to all people. In this case, you actually want to be a broken record. As the saying goes—"Play it again, Sam."

And speaking of broken records, nowhere is Impact Booster #4—Repetition more aptly exhibited than in the music industry. Take, for example, the meteoric rise to fame of Lady Gaga. While it is easy to question her outlandish costumes, her repetitive lyrics, and her over-the-top media stunts, it is hard to ignore her obvious musical talent and her ability to be at the right place at the right time with the right tune. Whether you love or hate her (and 99% of you are definitely in one camp or another), it is difficult to ignore the tremendous achievements of this branding genius.

In 2008, she was virtually unknown, and today she has several platinum selling albums and is the envy of artists that have been in the business for decades. In an industry cluttered with talented artists and interesting material, somehow SHE has managed to rise above almost everyone else and command our undivided attention.

Lady Gaga has got some really interesting songs but when you actually look at the lyrics—they are incredibly childlike and simple. In fact, she often repeats the same words or sounds over and over again. Her song "Bad Romance" is a great example of this as she repeats several key words, including "love", over and over.

Okay, Lady Gaga, we get it already, you want our love. And love (to her) likely means HUGE album sales, 30 million Twitter fans or just—money, money, money! After all, didn't ABBA drill that phrase into our heads in the 1980s and teach us that it's a rich man's world?

Chapter 18

So we all know that repetition works to sell music but why is it so powerful in business? Repetition is crucial to Sales Seduction because it helps your prospect remember your message and act upon it. If your message is memorable, your audience is ten times more likely to take action. That's why so much time was dedicated in Part 1 of this book to laying the foundation to capture attention and enhance recall with Old Brain Stimuli 1 through to 7. For those of you who have already mastered the 7 Stimuli That Charm the Old Brain, Impact Booster #4—Repetition can help you take your retention and results to the next level.

> **KEY POINT**
> **Having a message that is memorable boosts the likelihood that your audience will recall it and take action by ten times.**

So what role exactly does repetition play in enhancing memory? Is it really crucial to the process of embedding your sales and marketing message in the minds of your prospects?

Memory is simply the process of retaining and recalling information or experiences. It is the way that your brain takes in messages or facts, and stores them (either in short or long-term memory) for later retrieval or use. Short-term (or working) memory is the recording of information that is being used by the brain right now. Baddeley and Hitch, who calculated the short-term memory span, found that it can only contain (at any one time) three to four chunks of information in the form of letters, words, digits, or numbers. Unless repetition of this information occurs, it will be lost after about 20 seconds and will never be transferred to long-term memory. If your message is not transferred to long-term memory, it becomes virtually impossible to get your audience to recall it and take action.

The capacity for long-term memory, however, is theoretically unlimited. Once stored, the information can be retrieved by you at any time, with varying degrees of difficulty. That is because some sections of long-term memory are permanent while others tend to weaken over time.

For example, procedural memory includes motor skills such as learning how to tie your shoelaces, ride a bike, or drive a car. These memories are slow to acquire and once stored in long-term memory are very resistant to change or loss. Similarly, episodic memories (the record of events that you experience during the course of your lifetime) tend to be filed in long-term, permanent storage.

Declarative memory, however, is entirely different. The long-term memory facility that you use to recollect facts, names, places, and marketing messages is easier to access than the ones that hold your procedural and episodic memories. This means that you can acquire these declarative memories relatively quickly and easily but that you also lose them at the same rapid rate. This is where repetition becomes imperative. But how do you know when and how often to repeat your message for optimal retention?

A leap forward in the study of the optimum spacing for repetition came with the discovery of the Spacing Effect. We now know that learning and long-term memory is significantly improved when repeated information is distributed over time as compared to consecutively (massed repetitions in a very short space of time).

However, there is a distinct trade-off between time and memory. Once the space between the intervals reaches a critical point, the initial memory trace becomes inaccessible. Your brain will start at the beginning and treat the information as if you'd never seen it before. This means that **the optimum time between repetitions is likely to be the longest interval that avoids loss of the initial memory**. The difficult task for you as a marketer is to determine what that longest interval is—how much time can pass before your audience needs to be reminded of your claims and proof. Or stated another way, how much time can you afford to let pass before your prospect forgets your initial message completely?

Chapter 18

No one knows definitely why the Spacing Effect happens. Most believe that when your audience is only exposed to your message in short, consecutive bursts, the initial presentation remains within the short-term memory buffer during the onset of the second exposure. Because the working memory is still holding onto the message at the time of the second exposure, it does not require separate encoding and the benefit of repetition is diminished completely. It is also highly possible that during spaced or distributed exposure to your message over time, the retrieval cues in the brain of your prospect are more likely to be diversified and intensified.

Unfortunately, most of the research that has been done on successive repetition has focused on relatively simple memory tasks with equally spaced repetition schedules over relatively short periods of time—seconds, minutes, and hours. The introduction of one simple variation, for example a complex message with multiple parts, could drastically affect the conclusions reached by these leading researchers, and the implications for your message and your audience.

These limitations in the research make it difficult for someone like you to take these studies and use them to predict with accuracy what interval is best for your particular product or service, and your audience. In fact, it would be almost impossible for you to track and measure how frequently your audience is coming into contact with your sales or marketing messages.

That is precisely the reason why every time they see your message, you must capitalize on the opportunity to reinforce the valuable seed that you planted in their mind initially. You don't have the luxury of knowing when they last saw your message or asking them if they remember it. Therefore, you must take advantage of every chance you have to repeat your key messages and reinforce why your prospect should buy your solution. It is also another great argument for simplicity (Old Brain Stimulus #3—Is Your Message Concrete or Tangible Enough for a 6-Year-Old?). By keeping your message clear and uncomplicated, you increase the amount of time that may pass between successive repetitions of your message. You essentially buy yourself more time and decrease the likelihood your prospect will forget your message completely.

The truth is, your audience may need to see your message multiple times before they decide to contact you and take action. For those of you who have regular contact with your customers and prospects via newsletter, direct mail, blog, training seminars, or social media, you are increasing the likelihood that they are receiving enough touches to enhance their recollection of your key messages. But this only applies if you constantly reinforce those key claims and proof. If you choose to introduce new information each time you communicate with them, you lose the all-important benefit of repetition.

> **KEY POINT**
> Treat each encounter or touch point with your
> audience as an opportunity to reinforce the valuable
> seed that you planted in their mind initially.

Take our resident pet care and nutrition specialist, for example. Ben had invested a significant amount of time into drafting posts for his blog on a wide variety of pet related topics. Unfortunately, he had spread his efforts out so much that he had also attracted a whole lot of interest and traffic from extremists who had no intention of purchasing his products or services. In the pursuit to cover every pet topic imaginable, Ben did his business a huge disservice. He had the perfect vehicle to deliver a consistent message at regular 2-week intervals but he failed to reinforce and enhance his most important messages of all—his claim and proof that he could cure his customers' most important pain.

After all, Ben's ideal customer was as fanatical as he was about increasing the lives of their beloved pets. Ben's messaging around exercise and the right nutritional support for each individual pet really resonated with everyone who considered their little Fluffy or Spike to be "man's best friend". Ben

Chapter 18

understood that his customers hated the thought of their pet suffering or being unwell and they just wanted to do the right thing when it came to taking care of them. But that right thing changed from time to time with age and other factors, so they looked to Ben for guidance and support to put them back on the right path to their pet's optimal health.

Ben didn't claim to have the biggest range or the lowest prices. His primary claim was:

We are the leading expert in pet happiness and health.

If Fluffy is your best friend, we will show you how to help him live longer.

Armed with this knowledge, it only took 15 minutes to set Ben back up on the path to a healthier business. He had already laid the foundation to increase the frequency of contact with his customers via his blog and social media, he simply needed to make a few tweaks to rein in the breadth of topics he covered and ensure that his readers were getting a regular reminder of his key messages around health and nutrition. This new strategy and insight was also directly applicable to his other sales and marketing communications— in-store displays, brochures, newspaper ads, pay-per-click advertising etc.

In Ben's case, the changes started paying dividends very quickly. In addition to growing his leads and in-store traffic by 26% and his sales by 15%, he started to gain a sizeable following online and he was approached by a local radio station to do a weekly segment on pet care and nutrition. They were so impressed by the quality of his posts, they felt he would make an entertaining and knowledgeable guest for their lunchtime listeners on Fridays. By narrowing his focus and increasing repetition, Ben was able to magnify and multiply his results.

And remember, rarely will a customer act on your message the first time he sees it. If you want to earn his love and his business, you need to employ Impact Booster #4—Repetition. Once you have mastered the 7 Steps That

Help Your Prospects to Say "Yes", you are perfectly positioned to utilize this powerful impact booster. The key to predictable and reliable growth in your business is repetition—to maximize retention, you must re-iterate your most important message in your telephone greeting, brochures, business cards, website, social media accounts, press releases, thank you cards, and customer feedback surveys.

> **KEY POINT**
> Most prospects will not act on your message the first time they see it. Repetition is the key to reinforcing it in their long-term memory and giving you the best chance to earn their business when they are ready to buy THE solution.

Chapter 18

Why Do You Love a Good Mystery?

Impact Booster #5—Intrigue

Mandy doesn't have a face. She has many clients all over the world that have worked with her for years but most of them have never seen or met her. She's a VA (Virtual Assistant), one of the growing number of talented people whose office is the internet and who specialize in making the lives of others less complicated and stressful. With clients in different time zones, it's often tough to get her to step away from her desk. However, with a bit of coaxing and an offer she couldn't refuse, I was able to convince her to meet with me face-to-face.

CHAPTER 19

"Ah, it's good to get out for a change," Mandy sighed, as we settled at a sunny terrace table. "It's great, I've just got to the stage in my business where I have automated a lot of processes and can forward enquiries to others so that I can finally take a little time out for myself."

I had noticed that Mandy looked a little more rested than she did the last time we caught up.

"What kind of hours are you working?" I asked.

"Well, it's a bit sketchy at the moment," Mandy replied. "As you know, I'm juggling clients in several time zones and I don't have a set number of hours that I work each day. I'm still building up my business and my reputation so I'm burning the candle at both ends to get all the work done. You know, if a client needs something at five o'clock in the afternoon in London and I'm ten hours ahead, it means I've got to stay up until the wee hours to respond."

"It sounds like you're often operating round the clock," I said. "What sort of work do you do for these clients?"

"Oh, it could be anything," Mandy laughed. "I might be sourcing accommodation for a relocating family, supplying lists of PR websites, looking for bloggers that review certain products, data entry—anything really. And that's on top of my local clientele where I man two online support desks, provide transcription services, and help out with book launches and events for a few authors. I have requests coming in 24/7 and I have to work hard to organize and compress it all into a manageable 8 to 9-hour day."

"Phew! I'm tired just thinking about it. How do you find the time to do it all and sleep?"

Mandy laughed.

"It's not easy. But as I become busier, I bring extra resources on board to share the load. Just a few months ago, I hired another person in the Philippines to back me up with some of the transcription, online research, and writing. It allows me to focus on the work I prefer *and* have a bit more time to spend with my daughter. I'm in a transition phase right now—I just have to lift the income a bit more to keep everyone busy, that's all."

"So, how do you get your business now?" I asked.

Mandy flipped open her tablet and typed a couple of keywords into the search engine.

"There!" she said, pointing to her Google AdWords campaign. "That's me. The rest is word-of-mouth. I'm earning a great reputation with my regulars and they are happy to recommend me to their friends."

"Hmm," I said, staring at the long list of VAs advertising their services. "You've got a lot of VAs competing with you for pay-per-click ranking."

"Oh, they come and they go," Mandy said, nodding. "After all, anyone with a computer at home can set themselves up and advertise. It's getting and keeping the business—that's the hard part."

"Everyone sounds well staffed, inexpensive, and versatile," I said, running my eyes down the long list of similar ads.

"That's the problem," Mandy agreed. "I've been in this business for long enough to know that I can deliver. Unlike some of the newbies—many of them make grandiose claims about their abilities and command of the English language, then find themselves in deep water when they can't deliver on what they promised. It's not unusual for them to take your money and then disappear off the face of the earth. Most of my customers have had bad experiences before they found me online."

"How does your audience determine who's good and who isn't?" I asked. "Most of them look pretty good on paper."

"That's a great question that I don't know the answer to," Mandy confessed. "I guess it's a bit of a mystery."

When it comes to matters of the heart and seduction, as we discovered with Molly and Stella at the beginning of this book, wooing the object of your affection has little to do with conscious thought and rational processes. It has to do with primitive instincts and unconscious urges that happen below the surface of your awareness. You are attracted to certain people (and messages) and you act, long before you have the opportunity to think things through clearly. Rational thought takes place long after the decision has already been made by your old brain.

Oftentimes your heart and mind obey the laws of common sense. Typically, if you like me, I will almost certainly like you back. If you are rude or disrespectful to me, in all probability I will act the same way to you in return. We tend to respond in kind and, therefore, sociologists have termed this phenomenon the Reciprocity Principle, and it has been tested and proven in numerous studies.

However, sometimes your heart and mind defy this accepted principle and common sense, in both relationships and in business. That's where things get interesting and messy.

A number of researchers have recently surmised that when you and I are confident of a positive outcome (for example, that our liking or affection toward each other will be reciprocated equally), we tend to grow complacent in our thoughts and actions toward each other. On the other hand, if you are uncertain or insecure regarding my feelings of fondness toward you, you will find yourself hard pressed to think of or focus on anything else. My indecisiveness or vagueness will leave you strangely drawn toward me.

In 2010, a study by Whitchurch and Wilson examined this phenomenon by presenting 47 women on Facebook with a selection of profiles of men who indicated they (1) liked them best, (2) liked them an average amount, or (3) were uncertain whether they liked them at all. The results showed that the women felt more attraction to the males who liked them best as compared to those that indicated they only liked them an average amount. What was most surprising, however, was the fact that the women reported being the most attracted to the men who were uncertain about whether or not they even liked them in the first place. Those in the last (uncertain) category produced the strongest attraction ratings and generated the most positive mood amongst the participants. Apparently, it really does pay to "play hard to get".

So you might be asking yourself, *"What does this have to do with making my message more irresistible to my audience?"* Well, nothing and yet perhaps everything.

Your brain is hardwired to respond to novelty. That's why Old Brain Stimulus #2—Contrast is so powerful. The old brain uses contrast to help it to decide what to focus on, to make rapid decisions, and to keep you alive. In the same way that your reptilian brain looks for the message that stands out and is different, you also are predisposed to intrigue and mystery. You don't want it all spelled out for you. Your brain releases a powerful surge of dopamine (a secretion which is linked to pleasure and also the encounter of something new) every time that you experience reward or satisfaction, following a brief period of suspense.

> **KEY POINT**
> **The old brain of your prospect is drawn toward intrigue and mystery.**

When someone tells you a story that intrigues and moves you, you lean in and beg to hear the ending. If someone asks you a fascinating question, you listen much more intently when you know that she is about to reveal the answer. When something important is obscured or hidden from you, it

Chapter 19

piques your interest and makes you even more determined to uncover the answer. The part of your mind that decides is incorrigibly curious.

Knowing this vital clue about how your brain operates, I want you to ask yourself this question, *"Does my last sales and marketing message tickle the inquisitive mind of my prospect?"* If I were to pick it up and read it right now, would I be drawn in and compelled to probe you for more information? Or have you pretty much spelled it all out for me and ruined the surprise?

When you assess your message honestly, does it lull your audience into complacency or make them want to "like" you more and uncover HOW you can cure their greatest pain? The more competitive your marketplace is, the more vital this particular impact booster is to create campaigns that close more business.

Take Mandy, for example. She's in a cutthroat industry where most of her customers are buying on blind faith. In most circumstances, her customers never actually meet with her face-to-face and it is customary to ask for payment up-front. Her audience is drawn in solely by what they see in her ads and on her website. And if you do a quick search online right now you will discover that it is virtually impossible to tell her competition apart. They all went to the same school of copywriting and are focusing on the number of VAs they have on staff, hourly rates, experience, or where they are based. Here are some typical ads:

Online Asst. From $3/hr

Browse 9000+ online assistants.

Hourly/fixed. Get quotes today!

Find Virtual Assistants

Search 45,000+ virtual assistants.

Post your project. Get free quotes.

Outsource to Philippines

Outsource services to our Filipino

Virtual assistants. Contact us!

Not Sure Who to Trust?

We're the leading provider of VAs

Fixed/hourly, all work guaranteed.

Mandy's original pay-per-click ad (the last one on the list above) was converting fairly well at 7% and $3.76/click. Unlike all the others, it addressed the number one pain that her customers were in and staked her distinctive claim in the market. However, it didn't leave much to the imagination, and it didn't pique the interest of most online browsers enough to make them want to click and find out more. In order to get her click-through rate up and her cost per click down, Mandy knew that her ad needed some fine-tuning.

Armed with the knowledge of how the old brain is captivated by anticipation and mystery, she was able to modify her ad and multiply her results in a very short period of time:

Need a VA You Can Trust?

How much more could you do if

We took care of all your admin?

In just 72 hours, Mandy saw her conversions jump to 17% and her cost per click drop to $2.87. Her prospects not only knew that she understood their pain, they also suspected she was different than all the rest and they were dying to find out more about her services. Google also rewarded her handsomely with a drop in her pay-per-click rate because her ads were deemed to be more relevant and appealing.

Chapter 19

This technique can be used by you in almost any sales or marketing message. It is easy to apply and has the potential to increase your results substantially when used in conjunction with the 7 Stimuli That Charm the Old Brain and the 7 Steps That Help Your Prospects to Say "Yes". Incorporate this impact booster in the stories that you tell your audience—leave some clues and hints that draw the listener into the story and prompt them to ask you how the story ends. By opening your presentation or message with a fascinating question, you grab the listener up-front and leave her waiting, listening for, and anticipating the answer throughout. When you deliberately obscure or hide an important fact from your audience temporarily, it piques their interest and increases their resolve to uncover the answer.

Curiosity is like an aphrodisiac for the part of your brain that decides. To attract more customers and close more sales, you must cover the basics by mastering the 7 Steps in the Sales Seduction Process, but always leave your audience wanting more.

> **KEY POINT**
> **The part of the brain that decides is hopelessly curious. To boost your influence and persuasion, your message should include just enough to draw your prospect in, but not so much that you ruin the surprise.**

Do You Want to Get Ahead of the Curve?

Impact Booster #6—Curves Are Sexy

Lynn is one of my favorite people. Managing a plant nursery is extremely physical work and Lynn, wearing her trademark bright red boots, cut-off jean shorts, and halter top, manages to combine horticultural genius with a cheeky tomboy image that really appeals to her inner-city customers. As I strolled onto the premises, she gave me a cheery wave from behind a huge sack of something heavy that she was lugging deftly across the yard.

CHAPTER

"Have a look at the new extension and I'll pop the kettle on and join you in a moment," she called, charging off in the other direction.

The nursery was in full bloom. Teeming with healthy plants, flowers, and vegetables, it was a cornucopia of color. Lynn knew her stuff and had been involved in the industry for 25 years. She first stepped foot in the business at the ripe old age of six and she was her dad's little helper from then on, after school and on every weekend. On his retirement last year, he'd proudly handed the reins over to his ambitious daughter and she was keen to expand on what they had built together.

Just inside the newly developed annex, I paid the price for not paying attention to where my feet were treading. While busy admiring a stunning display of lush pink chrysanthemums, I grazed my arm on a piece of wood trellis jutting out dangerously across the walkway. Reacting quickly as I felt the searing pain, I then managed to catch a few innocuous scratches as I backed up into the rose bushes behind me. It just wasn't my day.

"What's happened?" Lynn asked, fighting through the underbrush as she came up the narrow aisle. "I heard someone call out. Are you okay?"

"I'll live," I laughed, dabbing some drops of thick red blood off my arm with a scrap of tissue that I found in my handbag. "I was just enjoying the beautiful fragrance of these chrysanthemums and I must not have been paying attention to where I was walking."

Lynn nonchalantly smiled as she unhooked a climbing rose's trailing tendril from the sleeve of my jacket.

"Well, it seems as if the plants have taken a liking to you anyway," she chided. "I absolutely have to show you this new shipment of baby palm trees that just came in. Follow me."

Lynn darted down another aisle, threading her way expertly between arrays of spiky bromeliads, cacti, and succulents. I followed behind carefully, shuffling sideways and steering well clear of the overhanging branches and leaves spilling out onto the pathway. They looked lush and harmless enough—the bright green leaves and intense red highlights were gorgeous— but I knew from experience that they could pack a sharp punch and these little fellas were getting a bit too close for comfort.

"I've tried on purpose to make the place really intimate and just a little bit wild," Lynn told me when I caught up. "I've seen too many sparse, formal looking nurseries in the big discount and hardware chains. You know the ones—straight lines with everything evenly spaced on rustic wooden pallets. Not natural looking at all."

"Is the new look working out for you?" I enquired while taking it all in visually.

"Oh, it will, I think," Lynn replied tentatively. "This place has been the same for years and people generally take some time to get used to change. A few of the younger customers have said that it feels more like a national park than a typical store or nursery. That seems like a positive response. But what do you think?"

"Lynn, I'm going to be straight with you," I replied with a smile. "Your selection is fantastic but this place feels a bit like a jungle to me, and if I didn't have you to help me navigate it safely, I'd be nervous about getting out in one piece."

Every day you walk into at least one retail location. It might be a grocery store, a gas station, a coffee shop, or the convenience store down the road from your home. And when you do, you know exactly what you like—what feels right and what doesn't. Some environments just feel instantly more inviting and comfortable than others, don't they?

The truth is, your level of ease and exhilaration are not determined by what you are aware of consciously, but rather by a whole lot of factors below the surface of conscious awareness. Those who are in the business of store design and merchandising know this better than anyone. They specialize in designing and manufacturing surroundings where your old brain feels safe and comfortable. And most of the best practices in this industry are based on neuroscience.

According to the CEO of NeuroFocus, a company in California that specializes in research that taps into the brains of potential customers, "the brain loves curves and detests sharp edges". In the exact same way that your caveman ancestors avoided or were fearful of spears, jagged teeth, and rocks fashioned into cutting devices, you have a strong innate aversion response to sharp edges, angles, and pointy objects in your environment. You view them as a potential threat to your safety and well-being at a deeply subconscious level.

Many of the neuro research companies have recently reported doing sizeable studies for retailers and food manufacturers in the US and the UK to test whether shoppers prefer in-store displays and packaging with rounded edges. However, most of the brands involved insisted on anonymity. It is, therefore, very difficult to assess the veracity of their claims that sales increases of 15–50% were achieved with merchandising and designs that employed curves. With any luck though, in the next few months we will start to see more revealing and candid studies on this topic published in journals by university based research teams.

> **KEY POINT**
> **The old brain loves curves but views sharp edges**
> **as a potential threat to safety and security.**

One such study by Angela Attwood at the University of Bristol sheds some light on the effect of curves in the packaging of alcoholic and non-alcoholic beverages. The first group of subjects, who were unaware their consumption was being monitored, were given a glass of beer before being asked to watch a short documentary film and answer a few questions. While all the glasses contained a half pint, some were straight sided, while others were fluted with a distinct curve. A selection of the group were served in a fluted glass, while others drank from the straight one.

The participants who were offered the straight glass took 60% longer (nearly 12 minutes in total) to finish their beverage than their counterparts who drank out of curved glasses. This effect was only observed when the subjects were given a full glass of beer and it was not borne out in the subjects who were given non-alcoholic beverages. The researchers then went on to make some hypotheses about why the subjects favored the curved shape and why it tended to accelerate consumption. They attributed at least part of the anomaly to the perceived difficulty in estimating the halfway point in the curved glass. Based on the assumption that a subject might naturally want to pace himself while drinking alcohol, it is believed this may have impacted the ability to judge the halfway point accurately with the curved glasses.

But all of this research that suggests that the brain loves curves in design, merchandising, and packaging still doesn't answer the all-important— WHY does the brain prefer curves? The simple answer to that puzzle is that no one knows for sure. Although it is highly probable that in addition to risk avoidance, which we know is a key driver for the reptilian brain, the brain correlates curves with sex, fertility, overall health, and nourishment. To explore the accuracy of this explanation to our question, Dr. Steven Platek, a cognitive neuroscientist at Georgia Gwinnett College, asked a group of male subjects to rate the attractiveness of seven naked women both before and after cosmetic surgery undertaken to give them much more shapely hips. These operations were conducted to harvest fat from the waists of the females and redistribute it to their buttocks, thereby enhancing the curvaceous aspect of their figures.

While the men studied the photos, their brains were scanned by Dr. Platek's team. While the pre-operative photos generated measurable neural responses, the post-operative photos generated significantly increased activity in the part of the brain associated with rewards. These reward centers—the part of the brain usually activated by drinking and taking drugs—lit up when the waist to hip ratio was boosted by surgery. According to the findings, Platek and his team concluded that women with hourglass figures proved particularly stimulating in terms of feedback and neural activity. This study also seems to prove that the presumption that men judge attractiveness of the opposite sex by body fat and dress size alone is based on societal expectations and media propaganda. The tangible evidence of a hardwired predisposition to curves suggests that on some deeper level the subjects likely attributed the enhanced shapeliness to sex, fertility, good health, and the ability to carry healthy babies.

> **KEY POINT**
> In addition to being hardwired to keep you safe, the reptilian brain likely prefers curves to sharp edges because of primitive cues that correlate curves with sex, fertility, overall health, and nourishment.

So we now know this instinct your brain has to favor curves is innate, persuasive, and powerful. But how can you use it to supercharge your store layout, merchandising, packaging, product design, or marketing message?

Well, let's first examine how Lynn used this insight to transform her product offering, merchandising, and sales. Even though she had become personally attached to her new store layout and the dense, jungle-like atmosphere, she could see how it would be viewed by the old brain of her customers as unsafe or treacherous. She had grown up with an incorrect belief (that many retailers have fallen victim to) that you have to have a lot of stock on hand, with tightly packed aisles and shelves, to have a successful business and entice customers to buy. In fact, this is often not the case.

The first step for Lynn was to identify all the dead and slow moving inventory she had on hand. By getting rid of overstocks and plants that just weren't selling, she was able to buy herself some breathing room and free up the floor space she needed to re-merchandise the entire store. She began by rearranging all the plants and trees by height to cut down on space requirements and to prevent her customers from being inadvertently poked in the eye or arm while browsing. She removed or relocated all wood and metal fencing and shelving that had sharp or jagged edges. The continuity and organization began to pay rewards almost immediately as customers began to stay longer in-store to browse and the average basket size increased by 2.4 items.

She was also able to widen the aisles by 45% when she introduced tiered levels of pallets and round, dense ends for feature product at the end of each walkway. This gave a more organized and streamlined feel to the store without making it feel sparse or like one of her discount or warehouse-style competitors. Customer surveys, informal feedback, and sales figures confirmed that the customers both appreciated the new, more comfortable and inviting shopping environment, they also spent more. Thirty one percent more, in fact. While the total number of customers grew by only 2–3% over the next two months, sales went up considerably. When I next caught up with her, she was making plans to extend the annex to expand her range of outdoor sculptures, water features, and garden accessories. She had already spoken to an architect about a neuro-friendly design and was training up one of her nieces to take over the merchandising efforts so she could concentrate more on sales and marketing.

Before moving on to the next chapter, take a moment to make a list of the key areas in your business that need to be redesigned or modified to appeal to the old brain of your prospects and customers. For those of you who have physical locations, reconsider your layout, selection, and merchandising to remove sharp edges and angles that may be perceived as uninviting or harmful. Pay particular attention to the design of your products and

Chapter 20

packaging. Does it feel nice in your customer's hands? How could it be adjusted or improved to make use of what you now know about the impact of curves on the old brain? When in doubt, look to other successful brands in the marketplace for ideas and inspiration. And finally, re-examine your marketing collateral and your website to identify opportunities to soften the edges of your message, the method of delivery, and your overall presentation.

KEY POINT

Your customers have a strong innate aversion response to sharp edges, angles, and pointy objects in your design, packaging, merchandising, and presentation. They are viewed as a potential threat to safety and well-being at a deeply subconscious level.

Can I Have That to Go?

Impact Booster #7—Leave Them With a Take-Away

Kylie and James, a husband and wife team, have been in the travel game for 15 years. I spoke to them recently about the changes they've seen in the industry as a result of the internet and was staggered to discover just how much their sales have been impacted by technology.

"It's amazing," Kylie said, as we sat down for lunch. "It only seems like yesterday that we sat across the desk from our clients with pen, paper, and a colored brochure in hand, and planned out their dream holidays."

"And now?" I asked.

CHAPTER 21

Kylie looked at James and laughed.

"We hardly see our customers in person. Most of them just call to let us know they are thinking of taking off for a little break and they ask us to put something together. You know, not too many people have the time to just drop in and see us anymore. Except, of course, on weekends—when they've got the whole family in tow!"

"And then it's a madhouse," James interjected, helping himself unabashedly to a second piece of bruschetta. "There are a lot more tire kickers and not enough staff to help everyone properly. Some just come in to get the glossy, colored brochures from the big travel companies, and then they go home to do their own research and book the flights and hotels direct online. You should see us on a Saturday—crazy, busy running around and not a minute to stop and grab a simple bite to eat."

"I see you are making up for lost opportunity today, honey," Kylie said, poking James affectionately in the stomach and turning back to me with a grin. "James is right, although I think it's a bit more complicated than that. Over the years we've been gradually losing our loyal clients, and the phone calls during the week are trailing off."

"What's the cause, do you think?" I asked.

"Well, the competition online from the airlines and big name travel discounters is really fierce. It puts pressure on all the agents to drop their prices, which means it's even harder for us to make a living and cover our costs of operation. Of course, the airlines can offer great deals because they get bigger commissions than we do to lock in car rentals and hotels, and the large franchise agencies have bulk buying power that we just can't compete with."

"Is the economy causing some of the slowdown?" I asked.

"Strangely enough, no," Kylie said thoughtfully. "International travel is down a bit but domestic excursions, especially beach holidays, are way up.

The pressure and stress of work seems to have made vacations even more important to our clientele. They don't want to waste their valuable days off lazing around home or taking care of domestic chores. They've worked hard and they want the reward of getting away—far away—to make the most of their time off. They'll even cut back on discretionary items and retail therapy if they have to, to preserve their annual holiday budget."

"The bottom line," James said, "is that everyone is so web savvy now. They can plan an entire holiday themselves—do their research, look for deals, see reviews, and book online—from their computer, tablet, or even their smart phone on the train to work. Why do they need us?"

I looked at Kylie and raised my eyebrows.

"Because we know how important the holiday is to them and their family, and booking with us gives them peace of mind. We do all the hard work behind the scenes to minimize risk and ensure they will come back with the best possible memories," Kylie countered. "Everyone knows that a self-designed holiday seems simple enough on the surface. But, when it comes to dealing with tight deadlines, knowing which carriers have the least amount of delays and cancellations, and giving sound travel advice, our 15 years of expertise has saved our customers a lot of grief, hassle, and money. We don't get regrets or complaints. Mostly, our customers come back in to show us their treasured holiday photos."

"Yup, lots of them, and always on Saturdays," James chuckled.

If you speak to anyone in the retail game—selling travel, fashion, electronics, books etc.—they will tell you that the internet has had a dramatic impact on their business. Whether the effect is perceived as positive or negative, however, depends on what the business owner themselves has done to react and adapt to the changes in their trading environment.

"The internet is killing my business" is a common cop-out that is used to deflect attention from the real issue. Truth be told, it is easier to blame declining revenue or failure on the internet than it is to step back, re-group, and adapt to the changes in a way that maximizes the impact and influence of what you have to offer. Every business faces disadvantages and obstacles. The brands that succeed over the long term are the ones that consistently captivate attention, amplify recall, and trigger a decision in every medium their message is communicated in.

The internet is simply a delivery channel. It hasn't made or broken anyone's business. If your sales or marketing message is inherently weak or ineffective, the internet cannot save it or magically transform it into a customer magnet. Conversely, if your message and your solution are strong, they will work (with minor adjustments) in any medium or channel. Your success (or lack thereof) is solely dependent on your ability to influence and push the "buy button" in your prospect's brain by speaking the language of seduction. It's about mastering the 7 Stimuli and the 7 Steps and applying the most appropriate Impact Boosters to every interaction you have with your prospects and customers.

> **KEY POINT**
> A strong message or solution, crafted using the language of Sales Seduction, will successfully push the "buy button" in your customer's brain no matter which channel you choose to communicate it in.

Unless your audience is deliberately deprived of one or more senses, what they perceive when they view your product, service, or message is always a multi-dimensional experience. Even though the old brain is primarily a visual beast, the other senses—touch, sound, taste, and smell—have the power to radically sway what is perceived, remembered, and acted upon.

Take, for example, the sensation of touch. Neuroscience has proven that simply touching a product or trialing a solution can stimulate your desire to

Chapter 21

buy it and initiate a feeling of ownership. This is one reason why retailers and businesses that meet with prospects face-to-face have a distinct advantage over their online counterparts. Just picking something up and holding it in your hand is enough to inspire a sense of entitlement and possession in your mind. It's why fashion retailers strongly encourage you to step into the fitting room to try garments on and our car salesman Tom (Chapter 9) was so eager to get his prospect behind the wheel of the SUV he'd picked out for her. Good salesmen and marketers know that possession is nine-tenths of the sale.

It is much more difficult to replicate this sense of entitlement online because shoppers cannot physically touch your products or services—they can only see and imagine what they might feel like in their hands. Online sellers must, therefore, work harder to manufacture this feeling of ownership. The easiest way to do this, of course, is to use the technique that Alicia employed in Chapter 13 to promote her social media software—provide a free sample or a trial period. It allows your audience to touch and feel your solution, while simultaneously creating an environment where they feel as if they already own it.

If a trial is not possible, use words or video to draw the audience in and invite them to imagine themselves possessing the solution. Where possible, choose sounds and imagery that paint a vivid picture and compensate for the lack of touch. A carefully selected sound holds the power to magnify and enhance your audience's perception of words, images, and textures. For instance, if you need to convey roughness or strain, consider using the sound of sandpaper being scraped across wood or the sound of someone pulling a heavy object across the floor. Chances are, your audience will interpret the texture as rougher, or the task as more difficult, than if they only see the visual cue or touch your product.

While vision can tend to dominate the domain of the old brain, different textures can also have a direct bearing on both the strength of the imprint and the brain's reliance on one sense over the other. According

Chapter 21

to groundbreaking research conducted by Charles Spence in 2004, rough textures can lead to visual domination, whereas finer textures tend to encourage touch to come forward as the overriding sense. This means that it is very possible to manipulate the impact of your message on the old brain by introducing carefully selected tactile cues to either reinforce the dominance of visual cues or redistribute that emphasis to touch or feeling.

As Hugh discovered in Chapter 15, strong visual cues alone are often not enough. It is easier to sell a good night's sleep when your prospect also feels tired and has a strong sense of what it will feel like to curl up in a bed that is perfectly suited to cure her pain. Even with a traditionally low touch medium such as a catalogue or brochure, Hugh was able to maximize the impact of his message on the old brain of his audience by drawing masterfully upon visual cues and evoking a strong sense of feeling.

The role of touch should never be underestimated. Where visual cues are impeded or distorted, the sensation of touch takes on a dominant role. As you might remember, Bill the pharmaceutical rep in Chapter 8 was under significant pressure to present his products to Diane in under 15 minutes. He knew that he would be meeting with her face-to-face but he suspected from his previous strained encounter that he needed to do more than just deliver a strong visual message to charm her old brain. In order to captivate her attention and buy himself more time to deliver his solution, Bill used a prop—the pillow and prescription in a box—to introduce the element of touch. From the moment she first opened the box and held the prescription in her hand, she felt ownership of the solution and she connected with Bill and with his message on a very deep level. Without a doubt, she left the box, pillow, and prescription in her office and every time she glanced at it, Bill's solution to her pain was reinforced. And when he finally met with her in person, he didn't bother with a whole lot of PowerPoint slides—he placed his products in her hands one-by-one and deliberately triggered her desire to have them.

KEY POINT
Possession is nine-tenths of the sale. If you want to sell something, put it into your prospect's hands either physically or metaphorically.

Touch also has the power to move you to take action immediately. According to a recent study by Peck and Shu, your willingness to pay a relatively higher price for a product or service is directly attributable to whether or not you have actually touched or handled it first. It is incorrect to assume that customers are not willing to pay a higher price for a product or service offline. In fact, they often do. The amount they are willing to pay you for the solution is directly correlated to three factors: (1) the amount of pain they are in, (2) whether or not you can solve that pain, and (3) how adept you are at putting the solution into their hands so they can claim ownership now. Price only becomes a concern when you haven't correctly identified their pain, proved you can solve it, or placed the solution in your prospect's hands. If you want to get paid a price you deserve, you must deliver on all three factors. Impact Booster #7—Leave Them With a Take-Away is crucial for your success and also for the business of my clients Kylie and James.

Kylie and James definitely had their challenges and some stiff competition online, but they also had one strategy in their arsenal that held the potential to transform their message and give them an unfair advantage over the web based businesses: Impact Booster #7—Leave Them With a Take-Away. They instinctively knew that the customers valued the visual appeal of the glossy brochures and the high-touch service of having a stress-free holiday. They suspected an online booking was mainly about price and that the prospect was unlikely to receive much support or follow-up to reinforce their excitement about the upcoming trip. They also had evidence that the photos and memories of the holiday lived on in the minds of their customers long after the families returned from their trips and went back to their everyday lives. They just needed to deliver their message and solution in a way that maximized the visual and tactile appeal on the old brain. If they were able to do that, they knew that they could create a sense of ownership, trigger a decision to buy, and compete robustly with their online competitors.

I caught up with Kylie and James three weeks later to see how their new strategies were working. They had decided to set up each client that walked through the doors with a digital photo frame. Instead of giving away glossy travel brochures, they loaded up the digital picture frame with a selection of scenic photos, hotel properties, wildlife, and interesting excursions from the prospects' desired holiday locations. The prospects were then encouraged to take their digital frames home (or to their office), while the travel agent got some itineraries together, with indicative pricing.

By the time the agent got back to each prospect, they had usually fallen in love with a specific location and were even more eager to commit and get their holidays booked in and paid for. In the meantime, the digital photos gave the clients something to look forward to and hang on to while they anticipated their departure date. And most of them were thrilled to discover that they could keep their digital photo frame as a thank you from Kylie and James and use it to house their precious photo memories when they returned.

Not surprisingly, their conversion rate started to climb almost immediately from less than 10% to 63%. Where previously they would have struggled to get one shopper out of ten to book and pay, they started closing 6.3 out of ten people that walked through the door. These customers expressed a strong attachment to their photos and holiday plans, and they were far less preoccupied with price than the customers who contacted the agency via telephone or email.

Without investing an additional dollar in mass advertising, online marketing, or direct mail, Kylie and James were able to double their sales organically by delivering a strong visual and tactile message to their prospects. They didn't fall into the trap of trying to compete based on price and convenience with all the other online and offline agents. They focused

Chapter 21

on what they could do better than everyone else and they delivered their message and solution to the old brain of their audience with significant impact, recall, and ownership. Once the prospects held the solution in their hands, the sale was virtually inevitable.

And as for you and your business, it is safe to say that this final Impact Booster—Leave Them With a Take-Away—can play a significant role in enhancing the impact of your sales and marketing message. If you present to or meet with clients face-to-face, leave them with something tangible to take away. It doesn't have to be sizeable or expensive, it simply must reinforce your message or the stories you have shared and remind them why they need your solution. Where possible, consider also using video, music, or tactile cues to draw your listener in and bring the story to life. If you are able to leave something of meaning with your prospect, you increase your chances exponentially of them remembering and taking action.

If you deliver your message in a traditionally low touch medium, you'll need to work harder to convey feeling and tactile sensations. But as you discovered with several of my clients, this task is still very possible. Pay particular attention to the words and sound that you use to capture attention and convey your claims and proof. If there is a an object that most prospects will have in their immediate environment while they are reading your message (for example, a phone, computer screen, or a pair of glasses), work that object into your story or message and use it to your advantage. Plant the seed in their mind that will support and enhance your message every time they handle or pick up that object. Give them something tangible to hold on to and make it impossible for them to think of anything else but you and your solution.

> **KEY POINT**
> The sensation of ownership created in your prospect's
> mind when she holds your product or solution in the
> palm of her hands is a powerful aphrodisiac.

Bibliography

Attwood, A.S., Scott-Samuel, N.E., Stothart, G. & Munafò, M.R. (2012). Glass Shape Influences Consumption Rate for Alcoholic Beverages, *PLoS ONE* 7(8): e43007.

Baddeley, A.D., Thomson, N. & Buchanan, M. (1975). Word length and the structure of short-term memory, *Journal of Verbal Learning and Verbal Behavior* 14, 575–589.

Baron, Reuben M. & Kenny, David A. (Dec 1986). The Moderator-Mediator Variable Distinction in Social Psychological Research: Conceptual and Statistical Considerations, *Journal of Personality and Social Psychology*, 51, 1173–1182.

Blanchette, J-F. & Johnson, D.G. (2002). Data retention and the panoptic society: The social benefits of forgetfulness, *The Inform. Soc.*, 18, 33–45.

Boulenger, Véronique; Silber, Beata Y.; Roy, Alice C.; Paulignan, Yves; Jeannerod, Marc & Nazir, Tatjana A. (Jan 2008). Subliminal display of action words interferes with motor planning: A combined EEG and kinematic study, *Journal of Physiology-Paris*, Vol. 102, Issues 1–3, 130–136.

Braun, K. & Rubin, D.C. (1998). The spacing effect depends on an encoding deficit, retrieval, and time in working memory: Evidence from once-presented words. *Memory*, 6(1), 37–65.

Brown, J. & Fenske, M. (2010). *The Winner's Brain*. United States of America: De Capo Press, 219–161.

Challis, B.H. (1993). Spacing effect on cued-memory tests depend upon level of processing. *Journal of Experimental Psychology, Learning, Memory, and Cognition*, 19, 2, 389–396.

Dakin, Steven C. & Watt, Roger J. (Apr 3, 2009). Biological "Barcodes" in Human Faces, *Journal of Vision* Vol. 9 No. 4 Article 2.

Damasio, Antonio (1994). *Descartes' Error*, London: Random House.

Dooley, Roger (Aug 2012). The Neuromarketing Challenge: First Response, www.neurosciencemarketing.com

Ebbinghaus, H. (1964). *Memory: A contribution to experimental psychology*, New York: Dover. (Originally in 1885).

Ernst, M.O. & Banks, M.S. (2002). Humans integrate visual and haptic information in a statistically optimal fashion. *Nature*, 415, 429–322.

Fisher, Gerald H. & Foster, Jeremy J. (Oct 1968). Apparent Sizes of Different Shapes and the Facility with Which They Can Be Identified, *Nature*, 219, 653–654.

Glenberg, A. M. (1979). Component levels theory of the effects of spacing of repetitions on recall and recognition. *Memory and Cognition*, 7, 95–112.

Gottfried, J.A., Winston, J.S. & Dolan, R.J. (2006). Dissociable codes of odor quality and odorant structure in human piriform cortex. *Neuron*, 49, 467–479.

Greene, R. L. (1989). Spacing effects in memory: Evidence for a two-process account. *Journal of Experimental Psychology: Learning, Memory, and Cognition*, 15, 371–377.

Harris, J. L. (2008). Priming obesity: Direct effects of television food advertising on eating behavior and food preferences. *PhD thesis*, Yale University, New Haven, CT.

Harris, J. L., & Bargh, J. A. (2009). Television viewing and unhealthy diet: Implications for children and media interventions. *Health Communication*, in press.

Harris, J. L., Bargh, J.A. & Brownell, K. (2009a). The direct effects of television food advertising on eating behaviour. *Health Psychology*, 28, 404–413.

Helt M.S., Eigsti I.M., Snyder P.J. & Fein D.A. (Sep–Oct 2010). *Contagious yawning in autistic and typical development. Child Development*, 81(5),1620–31.

Hintzman, D.L. (1974). *Theories in cognitive psychology: The Loyola Symposium* (Solso, R.L., Ed.). Potomac, MD: Lawrence Erlbaum.

Kahneman, D., Ritov, I. & Schkade, D. (1999). Economic preferences or attitude expressions? An analysis of dollar responses to public issues. *Journal of Risk and Uncertainty*, 19, 220–242. Reprinted as Ch. 36 in Kahneman, D. and Tversky, A. (Eds.), *Choices, Values and Frames*. New York: Cambridge University Press and the Russell Sage Foundation, 2000.

Kahneman, D. & Frederick, S. (2002). Representativeness revisited: Attribute substitution in intuitive judgment. In T. Gilovich, D. Griffin and D. Kahneman (Eds.) *Heuristics and Biases: The Psychology of Intuitive Judgment*. New York: Cambridge University Press, 2002.

Kahneman, D. & Frederick, S. (2002). Representativeness revisited: Attribute substitution in intuitive judgment. In T. Gilovich, D. Griffin and D. Kahneman (Eds.) *Heuristics and Biases: The Psychology of Intuitive Judgment*. New York: Cambridge University Press, 2002.

Krug, D., Davis, T.B., & Glover, J. (1990). Massed versus distributed repeated reading: A case of forgetting helping recall? *Journal of Educational Psychology*, 82, 366–371.

Lacey, S, Stilla, R., & Sathian, K. (2012). Metaphorically Feeling: Comprehending Textural Metaphors Activates Somatosensory Cortex. *Brain & Lang.*

Lezak, Muriel D., Howieson, Diane B., Loring, David W., Hannay, Fischer & Jill H. (July 2004). *Neuropsychological Assessment.*

Li, W., Luxenberg, E., Parrish, T., & Gottfried, J.A. (2006). Learning to smell the roses: experience-dependent neural plasticity in human piriform and orbitofrontal cortices. *Neuron* 52, 1097–1108.

Liu X., Ramirez, S., Pang, P., Puryear, C., Govindarajan, A., Deisseroth, K. & Tonegawa S. (2012). Optogenetic stimulation of a hippocampal engram activates fear memory recall. *Nature*, 484, 381–385.

Ludlam, Kerry (Feb 2012). Hearing metaphors activates sensory brain regions, *Woodruff Health Sciences Center*, Emory University.

Maltz, Dr. Maxwell (1960). *Pyscho Cybernetics*, Psycho-Cybernetics Foundation, California.

McKone, Elinor & Kanwisher, Nancy (2005). Does The Human Brain Process Objects of Expertise Like Faces, *McGovern Institute for Brain Research and Department of Brain & Cognitive Science*, MIT Press, 339–356.

Nielsen, (2011). State of the Media: *Consumer Usage Report.*

Norris, Garrett, (2010). British Association's Festival of Science, University of Leeds.

Norscia, Ivan & Palagi, Elisabetta (2011). Rogers, Lesley Joy. ed. Yawn Contagion and Empathy in Homo sapiens. *PLoS ONE* 6 (12): e28472.

Parker, Andrew et. al., (2001). Moving Your Eyes Improves Memory, Manchester Metropolitan University.

Peck, J. & Shu, S.B. (2009). The effect of mere touch on perceived ownership, *Journal of Consumer Research,* 36, 434–447.

Platek S.M. & Singh D. (2010). Optimal Waist-to-Hip Ratios in Women Activate Neural Reward Centers in Men, *PLoS ONE* 5(2): e9042. doi:10.1371/journal.pone.0009042

Raghubir, Priya & Aradna Krishna (Aug 1999). Vital Dimensions in Volume Perception: Can the Eye Fool the Stomach? *Journal of Marketing Research*, 36, 313–326.

Renvoise, Patrick & Morin, Christophe (2007). *Neuromarketing: Understanding the "Buy Buttons" in Your Customer's Brain*, Nashville, Tennessee: Thomas Nelson, 25–39, 49–63.

Senju, A., Maeda, M., Kikuchi, Y., Hasegawa, T., Tojo, Y. & Osanai, H. (2007). Absence of contagious yawning in children with autism spectrum disorder, *Biology Letters*, 3(6), 706–8.

Spence, C. (2004). A multisensory approach to touch. Conference paper, The magic touch: touching and handling in a cultural heritage context. *Heritage Studies Research Group, Institute of Archaeology,* University College London.

Suh, J., Rivest, A.J., Nakashiba, T., Tominaga, T. & Tonegawa, S. (2011). Entorhinal cortex layer III input to the hippocampus is crucial for temporal association memory. *Science*, 334, 1415–2.

Yin, R.K. (1969). Looking at Upside Down Faces, *Journal of Experimental Psychology*, 81, 141–145

Wansink, Brian (July 1996). Can Package Size Accelerate Usage Volume? *Journal of Marketing*, 60, 1–14.

Wansink , Brian & Van Ittersum, Koert (Dec 2003). Bottoms Up! The Influence of Elongation on Pouring and Consumption Volume. *Journal of Consumer Research*, Vol. 30, 455–462

Whitchurch, Erin R. & Wilson, Timothy D. (December 2010). He Loves Me, He Loves Me Not: Uncertainty Can Increase Romantic Attraction, *Publication Journal: Psychological Science*, University of Virginia, Charlottesville.

Zurawicki, Leon (2010). *Neuromarketing: Exploring the Brain of the Customer*, London & New York: Springer Heidelberg Dordrecht, pp. 77, 85.

About the Author

Rhondalynn Korolak is a lawyer, chartered accountant, Master of NLP and Clinical Hypnotherapist. She has distilled the secrets to business success, hat she learned while working with Price Waterhouse Coopers, Max Factor, Village Cinemas, and Coles Group Ltd and produced a simple step-by-step process that you can apply to your business to boost your bottom line.

Rhondalynn is the author of On the Shoulders of Giants, Imagineering Your Destiny, and Financial Foreplay. She has appeared on CNN, BNET/CBS, Channel 7, Channel 9, Kochie's Business Builders and 3AW, and writes for Yahoo, MYOB, Fast Thinking, Sunday Life, Dynamic Business, Business Spectator and Australian Retailer.

Rhondalynn can help you put strategies in place to grow your bottom line and ensure that your customers would never think of going elsewhere. She is the leading expert on harnessing the power of your mind and using it to improve your financial results in business.

Rhondalynn speaks annually to thousands of entrepreneurs, sales professionals, senior executives, franchisees, sporting clubs, corporate employees, and industry association members on the principles of leadership, business acceleration, and mental toughness.

As an entrepreneur, Rhondalynn founded Imagineering Now Pty Ltd and Businest Pty Ltd to serve the growing demand for customized training and coaching based on leading edge, scientifically proven technologies. That mission is realized via seminars, proprietary online financial software, and coaching curriculums that ignite the quest for self mastery while offering practical and proven techniques to rise above challenges and realize your deepest dreams and potential.

Get to Know Rhondalynn

Follow Rhondalynn on Twitter

http://twitter.com/rhondalynn

imagineering
UNLIMITED

Visit Rhondalynn's Blog at **www.imagineeringnow.com/category/ blog/**

Become a fan of Rhondalynn Korolak and Sales Seduction on Facebook

http://www.facebook.com/RhondalynnKorolak

http://tinyurl.com/salesseduction

Curious to Know HOW to to Seduce & Influence More Prospects & Customers?

The big brands like Apple, McDonald's and Coca-Cola have been using these techniques for years and have obtained iconic status in our hearts and minds. If you're ready to generate more leads, influence your customer to decide quickly, and make price a non-issue, you can apply to join our next online program. In this 8-week course, Rhondalynn will:

- show you how to **claw back customers** from your competitors

- reveal where you are **wasting money** on ineffective sales and marketing campaigns

- help you **avoid rejection** and prospects that need to "think about it" and

- take you through the entire Sales Seduction Process so that you can **influence and seduce more of your prospects and customers**

Included in your 8-week online program and resource pack, is a wall size poster and detailed workbook that will help you visualize the Sales Seduction Process, 8 powerful webinars, live teleseminars with Q&A time, and a 1-on-1 session with Rhondalynn via Skype. Rhondalynn will show you how easy it is to take Sales Seduction and apply it to your message, your product or service, and your customers.

Apply online now!

http://imagineeringnow.com/products/seduction-influence/

34311836R00127

Made in the USA
Lexington, KY
01 August 2014